★CAMP★
FOXLEY

First published by
Brewin Books Ltd, 56 Alcester Road,
Studley, Warwickshire B80 7LG in 2005
www.brewinbooks.com

ISBN 1 85858 285 7

A Cataloguing in Publication Record
for this title is available from the British Library.

Typeset in Plantin
Printed in Great Britain by
The Cromwell Press

★ CAMP ★ FOXLEY

FRAN & MARTIN COLLINS

*Best wishes
To Janet

Fran and Martin*

BREWIN BOOKS

CONTENTS

	Introduction	vii
Chapter 1	Brief Encounter	1
Chapter 2	'Fear Our Rage'	6
Chapter 3	Target Practice	18
Chapter 4	12th U.S. Hospital Center	26
Chapter 5	99th General Hospital	32
Chapter 6	156th General Hospital	41
Chapter 7	156th General Hospital - American Red Cross	50
Chapter 8	123rd General Hospital - 'Nothing Like Home'	63
Chapter 9	123rd General Hospital - Superior Ratings	74
Chapter 10	A Million Dollar Wound	83
Chapter 11	123rd General Hospital - American Red Cross	92
Chapter 12	Recreation	103
Chapter 13	Anglo - American Relationships	115
Chapter 14	The Final Chapter of the 123rd	122
Chapter 15	Polish Refugee Camp	130
Chapter 16	Foxley Housing Estate	140
Epilogue	Gone But Not Forgotten	146
	Abbreviations and Terms	152
Appendix 1	Units known to have been at Foxley	154
Appendix 2A	Army Hospital Centers	155
Appendix 2B	U.S. Army Hospitals in U.K. August 1944	156
Appendix 3	Trains arriving at Moorhampton Station with patients for Foxley	159
	Acknowledgements	160

Vertical Photograph of Camp Foxley 1946
(English Heritage N.M.R. R.A.F. Photography).

INTRODUCTION

On September 3rd 1939 Neville Chamberlain reluctantly addressed the people of Britain to inform them that they were at war with Germany because of Germany's refusal to withdraw its troops from Poland.

Britain had been preparing itself for war for some time prior to this date. One of the provisions was to complete a Central Register of Accommodation. This register listed Stately Homes in Britain which could be used in a State of Emergency. It included such information as a description of the premises, the stage of emergency at which the premises were to be taken over and for how long and which department was to occupy the premises. The register was compiled in secret and the owner of the property was not informed.

On the outbreak of war some houses were requisitioned immediately while others were taken over later when more accommodation was required. Very few houses escaped requisitioning altogether. If the actual house was deemed to be unsuitable the parkland around the house was used for tented camps. More buildings and land were needed as foreign troops started arriving in large numbers in the United Kingdom.

Foxley Manor House and its surrounding parkland were requisitioned early in the war. The house, situated seven miles northwest of Hereford between the villages of Yazor and Mansel Lacy, was an eighteenth century structure virtually rebuilt in the nineteenth century by the Davenports of Davenport China. The estate consisted of roughly 2,500 acres of agricultural land. Timber was one of the main

Foxley Manor House.

products of the estate and Foxley had its own lumber yard. Foxley also incorporated several small holdings which were rented out.

The first military occupation of Foxley was by a Canadian unit which built its own barracks in the grounds from wood shipped over from Canada. From the beginning of 1944 a number of American armoured and artillery units used the Canadian built huts as a temporary staging post while they prepared for combat on the Continent. In another part of the parkland work was commenced to build two purpose built hospital plants to house casualties from the proposed invasion of Europe. Shortly after D-Day an American General Hospital unit moved into one of the hospitals for a few weeks until it left to set up a hospital on the continent. It was replaced by two hospitals units, which dealt with a large number of casualties from the continent over the next year.

Towards the end of the war German Prisoners of War were put to work on the camp, carrying out menial tasks at the hospitals. They lived in a stockade built near the Manor House and were policed by a number of Military Police Battalions which supervised their tasks.

The camp was vacated by the Americans in the Summer of 1945 and the buildings were made available to Polish refugees who built their own community there. In the 1950's squatters awaiting rehousing lived at the camp until Hereford City Council built more homes in Hereford.

This book sets out the history of the camp, the part it played in the progress of the war and its impact on the surrounding area and its inhabitants.

Chapter 1

BRIEF ENCOUNTER

In December 1939 the 1st Canadian Division arrived in Britain. This division was based at the British Army Barracks in Aldershot. In the summer of 1940 it was joined by the 2nd Division and in July 1941 the 3rd Division.

From 1940 a number of Canadian units were based at Foxley. The first group to arrive was the 2nd Canadian Pioneer Battalion. It used the Manor house for billets and started to build a military camp in the grounds. The battalion had wood shipped over from Canada to build the huts, which were built on land around the manor house and in the woods around the house.

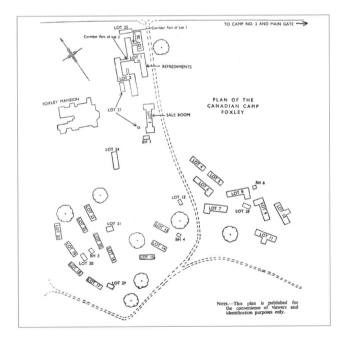

Plan of Canadian Camp at Foxley (Hereford County Records Office).

2nd Canadian Pioneer Battalion in Canada prior to shipment to U.K.
(L. Goodwin).

Hank Norton of the 2nd Canadian Pioneer Battalion with Betty and Joy Merrick in their garden at Mansel Lacy (L. Goodwin).

This unit only stayed at Foxley for a few months and then moved on to the south of England. Members of the 2nd Pioneer Battalion soon got to know the local area, often walking to the Moorhampton Hotel in Moorhampton where they would be served cider. Some of the unit attended a dance in Mansel Lacy Village Hall where one of the men, Dick Children, met a local girl called Betty Merrick. Romance blossomed and the date of 25 October 1941 was set for the wedding. By this time Dick's battalion had moved down South so it was necessary for him to travel back to Mansel Lacy where the wedding took place in the small Parish Church.

Betty's family all helped to provide for the wedding. Betty made her own wedding dress with material, which her sister, Joy (who worked in the fabric trade) was able to acquire. Betty's mother provided the food for the reception and even made a wedding cake, although it had no icing. Several of Dick's friends from the 2nd Pioneer Battalion attended the wedding including Hank Norton, who was the best man. After the war Dick returned to LePas, Canada to be demobbed and visit his family before returning to Herefordshire to farm, which he did until his retirement.

After the Pioneer Battalion left Foxley more Canadian units moved into Foxley Camp. It is possible that these units were attached to the R.C.A.F. and had connections with the nearby R.A.F. base at Credenhill.

Twenty year old Eileen also recalls a chance meeting with a Canadian based at Foxley. Eileen lived in the nearby town of Kington. She remembers it as a quiet market town with a busy railway station, two quarries, two building firms, surrounded by farms. In her words:

"War broke out, everything altered drastically."

In 1940 evacuees poured into the area from Liverpool, then a large number of soldiers were evacuated from Dunkirk and housed in tents in fields around the town. Eileen met and fell in love with Ieuan Walters, a soldier from the 2nd Battalion Essex Regiment. The couple set a date to marry on 5 July 1941.

Wedding of Dick Children and Betty Merrick at Mansel Lacy Parish Church (E.Children).

Meanwhile Ieuan's unit left for Brighton for training. In June he had leave and was able to travel from Brighton to Hereford. Eileen set out early in the family car to meet him at Hereford Station. She recalls her journey:

"Along the Hereford Road early in the morning and not a soul in sight, I came across a soldier lying in the road. In these days I would not have dared to stop but it was different then. I thought he was drunk, but when I went to him he looked ill, he just said, 'Foxley, Foxley'. How I got him in the car I will never know but I drove him to Foxley and spoke to two officers. They promised to let me know if he recovered. I told them that was all I wanted to know because I was getting married on 5 July. I went on and met my fiancé. I did not mention the incident to him or my family.

"A fortnight later an army lorry pulled up outside my father's shop in High Street, Kington, two soldiers came to see me. They told me that the soldier I delivered was suffering with a perforated ulcer and was very ill but would recover. They wanted to form a 'Guard of Honour' at my wedding and they made me a beautiful Hope Chest (which is equal to an English Bottom Drawer). I was quite overcome. We chatted for some time and they understood that I could not accept the Guard of Honour, my fiancé had only known me a few weeks and would never understand how I knew all these soldiers, after all I was a quiet country girl. I gratefully accepted the Hope Chest and gave it to my niece, who was delighted."

Eileen's wedding went ahead on the set date, without the Canadian Guard of Honour, and the couple went on to have a long and happy marriage although they spent much of the war years apart. Ieuan was an anti-tank gunner who was presented the Military Medal by George VI for gallantry in Holland.

Other local people from Hereford recall seeing the Canadians around the city and remember seeing them singing in harmony on the banks of the River Wye. By 1944 all of the Canadian units had left Foxley.

Mansel Lacy Parish Church 2004 (M.Collins).

Chapter 2

'FEAR OUR RAGE'

After the Canadians had left, Foxley became a staging area for a number of American units in preparation for shipment over to France. The camp had a large hard standing where artillery and armoured vehicles could be parked. A number of the units based for a short time at Foxley were artillery or armoured battalions, which spent their time training in the Herefordshire countryside and the Black Mountain Range in Wales.

The 749th Tank Battalion arrived at Foxley in February 1944. This unit had travelled to Cardiff from New York aboard the former Grace Line Cruise Ship, S.S. Santa Paula. The ship, which had 2,000 men on board, was part of the largest convoy that had sailed from the U.S. up to this moment. Jim Bobbet of the 749th remembers that the convoy stretched out of sight to the North and the South. Bill McFaddon, also of the 749th, describes the sight:

"Daylight revealed that we had mixed into the largest armada of ships ever assembled. Liners, tankers, destroyers, cruisers, every type of seagoing vessel you could imagine were there. Occasional booms in the distance led us to know that the navy was protecting us." - 749er.

George Baker recalls the journey across the Atlantic:

"The seas were rough and submarines were known to be in the area. But we were in a huge convoy and did not get attacked. The accommodations were far from the best, hammocks were stacked five high. One quickly learnt the best hammock was the highest one because people would get sick and you would be out of the way of the cascade of food that would come down." - 749th Training in Texas and England. - D. Heathcott.

Bill McFaddon remembers that the bunks had fence wire strung between them and that the British Government would charge the U.S. $28 for any damage to these bunks.

Jim Bobbet belonged to 'A Company', which was incorporated into the ship's gun crew for the voyage. He remembers:

"The gun crew's first job was to load the 20mm shells into a cloth container belt making sure to put them in rotation of red for tracer, black for armor piercing, blue for fluorescence. It was hard for five guys to reach into a wood box for the ammunition so I just dumped all the shells onto the steel deck and we could all pick them up more easily. About this time the Navy lieutenant came by and shouted at us not to move or touch the ammo as they would explode if the noses were touched. The lieutenant was very frightened as he thought we were careless, so we did it his way." - 749th Training in Texas and England. - D. Heathcott.

The 749th had rough seas for their journey across the Atlantic. Jim Bobbet remembers that the storms lasted three to four days of the fortnight journey:

"The ships on either side of ours would disappear in the waves, then come barging up, towering over us, then disappear again." - 749er.

Because of the large numbers of troops on board and the amount of time it took to feed them, meals were served just twice a day. Jim remarks:

"With almost everyone seasick at one time or another there weren't many complaints about not having three squares a day." - 749er.

Bill McFaddon, however, did miss his food. He recalls:

"I never came as close to starving as I did on that trip. In the morning they'd give us a cup of what they called coffee - I think it had some lye in it. It wasn't fit to drink. At lunch they'd give you a piece of liver sausage. At supper they'd give you what must have been horsemeat - the more you chewed it, the bigger it would get.

They opened the P.X. on the boat every day and there would be a line so long that it would still be there when they closed the P.X. I saw candy bars selling for $5. Cigarettes were 55 cents per carton - no tax." - 749er.

Bob Pringle remembers that at one point you could buy an ice cream for 10 cents at the P.X, but the storm caused a two hour wait for a cone.

George Baker also recalls the meals as being unappetising:

"The cooks were oriental and prepared the food in steam kettles that were eight feet in diameter. The cooks were very sloppy and not too clean in the preparation of the food, and that, along with the rolling of the ship made the food not so appetising to say the least. I would say that at the end of that time (the sea journey) that we were in the worst physical shape - terrible food, no activities, no sleep, cold - the ship was not heated to any extent, salt water so no showers. Deplorable conditions." - 749er.

Bob Myers, another member of the unit, remembers that a large number of the men were very seasick. He befriended a Navy man who put a safety line on him so that instead of being inside the ship he could travel on deck and get some fresh air. Because so many were seasick it was necessary for the gun crew to do a stint of K.P. Jim Bobbet remembers having to break eggs into a garbage can sized pot:

"The sight of the shelled eggs shifting around sent me topside to the railing. I tried to go back to my K.P. duties but one look at the eggs and I would get sick again. Eventually I found a place topside where I could not see the ship bouncing around and where I recovered from my seasickness." - 749er.

While A Company were on K.P. duty there was some opportunity to 'liberate' some food from the Officer's Mess. Bill McFaddon and Jim Bobbet both remember roast chickens finding their way to the men's quarters. George Baker remembers acquiring food in a similar way:

"One of the guys assigned to get supplies up from the ship's hold was really afraid to go down there so we traded duties. My, what a lucky break that was for me. Each day for two weeks or so I helped bring up food supplies from the hold of the ship, the food lockers, the freezer lockers and the fruit storage area. This had to be done twice a day due to the fact that we were feeding such a large number of troops billeted in the State Rooms and the hold of the ship. The bakery for the ship was on the top deck and we had to bring the baked goods and bread from there to the promenade deck. During these trips we would occasionally 'acquire' fresh hot pies intended for the officers. While on this duty we saw to it that we were very well fed." - 749er.

While on board the men had to entertain themselves. They played 'craps' and cards. Because 18 year old Bob Myers was such a poor card player some of the other soldiers actually gave him money to shoot craps if he promised to play cards. He recalls:

"I'd win some money at craps and they'd take it back in cards. When I landed in Britain I didn't have enough money to buy my rations: a dollar and 20 cents." - 749er.

The Santa Paula landed at Cardiff on February 22, a dull day. Bob remembers that there was a band playing on the quay and that it was raining:

"just like it always was in movies about England. I said, I've been here before." - 749er.

The men were relieved to disembark at Cardiff but were surprised to find that they had a communication problem with the Welsh ladies they met, as they couldn't understand the accent.

On their arrival at Foxley the men were pleased to see that they were to stay in permanent buildings rather than tents although they did find the buildings rather sparse. Jack Morris describes them:

"Those miserable barracks had concrete floors and three very small coke burning stoves which never warmed the interior sufficiently." - 749er.

George Baker also recalls the inadequacy of the heating. The stoves were called space heaters but George remembers that the space they heated was only a six inch circle around the stove. He also recalls that the mattresses were stuffed with straw although he did not consider this a particular hardship. Loren Rosencrantz remembers that the plumbing for the camp was not very extensive and clothes had to be washed in an old rain barrel.

Photos of detachments of 749th Tank Battalion while at Foxley
(David Heathcott).

9

*Photos of companies of 749th Tank Battalion while at Foxley
(David Heathcott).*

The men were also unimpressed with the food served at the camp. During the time of food rationing and shortages in the U.K. mutton had become the staple diet. The Americans were unused to this and Troutman states that:

"They said that it was mutton but it tasted like horsemeat to me. I didn't go for it very much." - 749er.

Bob Cooley remembers that on one occasion the chef, Sergeant McLean, asked him to buy a dozen eggs in Hereford. Apparently the chef wanted to take the shells off and sprinkle them in the powdered eggs so the men would think they were being served fresh eggs.

Photos of Companies of 749th Tank Battalion while at Foxley
(David Heathcott).

Once the 749th's tanks had arrived at Foxley training could commence. Tank firing was carried out in the Black Mountains with live ammunition. The tanks fired out over St. Georges Channel. The 749th trained alongside the 745th and 747th Tank Battalions, together making up the 6th Tank Group, which were destined to go in with the invasion force on D-Day. The 749th were due to take part in the infamous training exercise for D-Day at Slapton Sands in Devon but the Commanding Officer, Colonel Donald Donaldson, came down with the a bout of the measles and the unit were left out of the exercise.

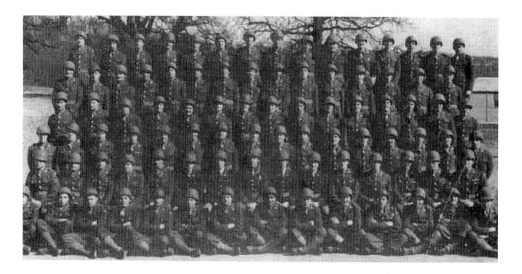

Photos of Companies of 749th Tank Battalion while at Foxley
(David Heathcott).

A number of the personnel of the 749th attended the exercise as observers. George Baker remembers that the sight was 'sickening to see' as two German submarines infiltrated the exercise and sank two ships, losing a large number of men. This was only one of the factors that led to the major disaster that the exercise became. When all the facts came to light years later it was said that there were more men lost in this training exercise than on Utah Beach on D-Day. Even General Eisenhower was said to have turned away from the spectacle. George comments that one positive result was that

Photos of Gordon Mize of the 749th whilst spending off duty Time in Hereford and Birmingham (Gordon Mize).

several changes for the better were made to the process of transporting and loading tanks as lessons had been learnt from the exercise.

In preparation for the invasion it was necessary to learn how to waterproof tanks. Steve Bodo recalls that a group of the 749th went to Brighton to 'waterproofing school':

"I drove a truck with Lieutenant Christensen from C. Company in charge. On the way back to camp he had me make a right turn. I heard a terrible sound. We stopped and found out that I had run into General Patton's Cadillac and put it upon the sidewalk. I think that was the only time that General Patton was speechless. I never heard any more about the accident, for which I was grateful" - 749er.

Some of the other men of the unit remember that there were a few 'near misses' when driving the tanks, particularly at night without headlights, until the men had got accustomed to driving on British roads.

The nearest town to Foxley was Hereford, which could be reached by bus. Several of the men from the 749th found that it was a long walk when they missed the last bus back to camp. George Baker felt that the English people in the town treated the Americans, (who he admits could be arrogant) well. He recalls that they tried to include the soldiers in their normal social events.

Some of the men from the 749th were asked to help with Military Police duties in Hereford. During the war there were white and black American units camped around the Hereford area. For a short while the 1310th Engineer General Service Regiment, which was an all black unit, was based at Foxley while the two hospital plants were being built. The black soldiers were accustomed to a policy of segregation in their own country and expected the same treatment in England. They didn't feel comfortable being served by the white girls in the transport canteen at Hereford Bus Station. White soldiers would sometimes push in front of the black soldiers because they thought they deserved to be served first. The English girls would usually refuse to do this and serve each soldier in turn as they came to the counter. This caused some ill feeling. Because of the American policy of segregation a system of 'white' nights and 'coloured' nights was set up in Hereford. George Baker remembers that there were some awkward situations as some of the local girls dated both the white and the black soldiers on their respective nights in town. He recalls that:

"- there was more than one casualty."

In February 1945 two white soldiers were stabbed by some black soldiers. The Hereford Times reported the incident:

"What happened apparently was that two white soldiers were in the canteen bent upon obtaining refreshments while waiting for a bus and there was a party of coloured U.S. troops there also. An altercation ensued and the canteen was cleared, following which the white soldiers were found to be suffering from deep wounds to the back. The injured men were removed to hospital and are understood to be making a good recovery.

"Detective Constable Cyril Naylor of the Hereford City Police Force has been engaged in assisting the American authorities in connection with the elucidation of this affair. He is anxious to trace the weapon with which the wounds were caused and asks us to make an appeal to anyone who has found a knife or any other sharp instrument in the neighbourhood of the bus station should hand it in at the Hereford City Police Office, Gaol Street" - Hereford Times 17.02.45.

The Hereford Times reported another case in the same month where the police were involved. This time they were looking for two white American soldiers who had murdered a civilian, Mr. Newman. Mr. Newman's son had found his father lying on the floor, injured, in Hereford on the evening of January 10. His father had told him that he had been attacked and robbed of his watch and chain. He said that the two soldiers had asked him for a light so he had given them some matches, then they had asked him the way to town. When he had given them directions they had hit him and he had fallen to the ground. When his son found him his face was covered in blood and he was bleeding from the back of his head. Two girls had seen the men running away from the direction of the bridge where the man had been found.

14

Mr. Newman died seventeen days later but at the time of the report Detective Constable Cyril Naylor had been unable to trace the alleged assailants even though he had made extensive enquiries at the American camps in the area.

A less serious incident at court regarding an American witness was reported by the Hereford Times on May 19 1945 under the heading:

"Any Gum chum. - During cross examination of an American soldier at the meeting of the Herefordshire County Quarter Sessions Appeals Committee on Monday a member of the bar experienced no little difficulty in catching what the witness was saying.

Eventually, after asking the witness on several occasions to repeat an answer to the council - did he have a twinkle in his eye? - inquired 'By the way have you anything wrong with your mouth?'

The elliptical motions of the witness's lower jar ceased - the lips shaped themselves into a smile. Another member of the bar made a suggestion which led the chairman to make the query - 'I suppose you can talk without chewing gum in your mouth?'

That indicated to the soldier the course of action desired of him. But getting rid of the offending morsel without infringing court decorum presented him with some difficulty. After some moments of concern in which he obviously turned over the possibilities in his mind, he withdrew the wad and held it in his hand during the rest of his evidence." - Hereford Times 19.05.45.

A couple of miles down the road from Foxley was R.A.F. Credenhill, where a detachment of W.A.A.Fs were stationed. Bob Myers remembers that the G.I.'s from the tank unit would often meet the W.A.A.Fs in pubs and walk them back to their base. He and his friend, Jim, would flip a coin:

" - to see who got the fat or ugly one, since the women always travelled in pairs too." - 749th Training in Texas and England - D.Heathcott.

At one point the W.A.A.F Commander came to visit Colonel Donaldson, the 749th's Commanding Officer. Jack Morris recalls:

"Their meeting was quite friendly and held with proper decorum until she stated the purpose of her visit. She simply asked Colonel Donaldson if he couldn't do something about the promiscuous cuddling the Yanks were engaging in near her girl's barracks. At that point the Colonel nearly choked as he had a to maintain a respectful and understanding attitude. Needless to say the event provided a good laugh and a warm remembrance for all concerned." - 749er.

After eighteen weeks at Foxley the unit was alerted to move out to Portsmouth. Bill McFaddon remembers that when they moved out it was dark outside:

"We went tearing down the road and I caught a telephone wire right in the mouth. The wire snapped - sounded like a ricocheting bullet. I cracked my head on the back of the turret. Cut my lips up pretty bad but they healed up just fine." - 749th Training in Texas and England - D.Heathcott.

As the convoy drove through Bath George Baker remembers that:

" - one of the tanks skidded on the cobblestones and rolled right over some poor guy's roadster parked at a pub. The people jumped out of the pub and screamed at us. We replied, 'See the guy at the end of the line. He'll sign your card!'"

At Portsmouth the tanks were parked on hard standings where they were waterproofed with a tar like substance. George recalls that they had to cover:

" - the entire tank, every inch, every bolt, every rivet hole - for water-proofing. We did not know if we would land on land or in three to four feet of water. Here you are - hands and clothes full of tar, gooey, sticky, tired, hungry - and there is no place to go. You're parked on these macadam lots. Sleep on the tank or sleep on the ground." - 749th Training in Texas and England - D.Heathcott.

The tanks were also fitted with 'bonnets' which kept the water out of the carburettor, these were to be discarded as the tanks landed on the beaches.

George remembers that the 749th were originally scheduled to go in on the first invasion wave, but again the C.O, Colonel Donaldson, was ill, this time he had been hospitalised. It was decided that the 749th would go when Colonel Donaldson could lead them. Again it was probably a lucky escape for the group as due to several unforeseen factors a number of tanks attempting to land on the American beaches on D-Day sank in deep water before they reached the beaches, drowning their occupants.

Tanks boarding L.S.Ts ready to go to France.

Left - Clem Osbourne of Company B. Wounded in France in December 1944 at which time he received the Purple Heart and Bronze Star (D. Heathcott).
Right - New M-4A3E8 Tank on bridge that collapsed with weight of vehicle during operation against Grosblieberstroff on the Saar. Tank is from 749th Tank Battalion. Dated February 18, 1945. Archive Number 111-SC-233735.

On June 27th, after an inspiring speech by General Patton, the tanks were loaded on the landing crafts. The Battalion were delayed for a day while the beach head was secured by the tanks that had made it to the beaches. Lead units of the 749th arrived on Utah Beach on June 29 as part of the 1st Army. George Baker recalls the day vividly:

"A scene of organised chaos. The foamy water was still blood tinged. We could see and hear the flashes of fire and see the smoke from the ongoing battles. Nearby German planes were still strafing the beaches. Barricades were still in place."

The 749th lived up to their motto: 'Fear Our Rage' when they first encountered action at St. Mere Eglise on 2nd July. Unfortunately a number of tanks and men were lost in the battle the next day. The battalion was integrated into Patton's 3rd Army as it moved through Europe.

The 749th Tank Battalion holds the record for an armoured unit for spending 196 days in combat. The men of the battalion travelled over two thousand miles with their tanks through France, Belgium and Germany. One of their elements, consisting of 3 light tanks, a half track and a jeep were part of the group that met and shook hands with the Russians in Czechoslovakia. During the campaigns on the Continent the 749th were part of three different armies and four army corps and served with nine infantry divisions, one armoured division and one cavalry group. The Battalion was finally inactivated on September 19 1945 at Camp Shanks, New York.

Chapter 3

TARGET PRACTICE

The 553rd U.S. Engineer Heavy Pontoon Bridge Battalion also arrived at Foxley in February 1944. This unit sailed from Boston, Massachusetts to Cardiff on the S.S. Exchange. From here the men were transported by truck to Foxley whilst their equipment went by rail. The equipment consisted of heavy pontoon equipment, foot bridge equipment and assault boats. To transport this the unit had 32 semi trucks, one of which was mounted with a crane. The semis carried 28 pontoon loads and four trestle loads. The unit also had two D6 tractors, four 2 1/2 ton G.M.C. trucks, four 4 ton trucks, one wrecker, six 3/4 ton Dodge Weapons Carriers and one jeep.

The 553rd were trained to build 25 ton reinforced bridges, which would be capable of carrying over 40 ton, easily accommodating the M4 Sherman tank, which was about 32 ton. This would be the heaviest U.S. vehicle likely to need to traverse the pontoon. Leo Wisniewski, a member of the 553rd, comments that nowadays U.S. pontoon bridges have to be rated over 60 ton to carry the M1A1 Abrams tank.

*Autocar semi trucks with pontoons on hard standing in
Foxley Wood 1944 (D. Stofer).*

Hard standing in Foxley Wood 1999 (M. Collins).

The 380 men of the 553rd were divided into 3 companies, They were billeted in concrete buildings that had been purpose built at Foxley for a hospital unit which had not yet arrived at the camp. The hospital plant included shower blocks and a mess hall on the Foxley site. There was a P.X where the men could buy personal items, Leo Wisniewski recalls that he often bought food there as:

"Being young (20) I never did get enough to eat."

Leo's first impressions of England was that everything was *'so green'* compared to Texas and Arizona where the unit had previously been training. Leo describes his training in England as:

" - getting into physical shape. We took long walks in the countryside, night compass training, scouting and patrolling."

Dave Stofer, also of the 553rd recalls:

"We spent our time at Foxley maintaining our equipment and physical well being."

Dave remembers being given target practice on the side of a hill near Foxley. Before the practice started it was necessary to go around to the other side of the hill to warn the residents. While at Foxley the men were also given training in German mines and booby traps.

Off duty time was spent in and around Hereford. The men attended and played in basketball and soccer matches with other units in the area. Boxing matches were arranged between the personnel of the nearby R.A.F. station at

Left - Personnel of the 553rd in front of barracks at Foxley (D.Stofer).
Right - 553rd Bridge erected on Moselle River, France (D.Stofer).

Credenhill and G.I.'s from Foxley. Leo Wisniewski recalls visiting Credenhill which he remembers as being *'plush'* in comparison to Foxley. The Americans were given a meal of beef, peas and potatoes which Leo recalls had no flavour or seasoning. Leo's impression of the British military was that they were *'polite'* but *'reserved'* and he felt that they didn't have much love for the American G.I. He believes that the expression *'Over paid, over sexed and over here'* sums up what the British Military personnel thought of the G.Is and he felt that this was understandable given the behaviour of some of the G.Is in Britain.

The 553rd left Foxley around D-Day. Each company moved to smaller camps around Hereford. H.Q. and Service Company moved to a camp called Brickfield. Leo recalls that B.Company bivouacked at Bridge Sollers on the River Wye and he remembers sitting and watching the swans there. The Battalion kept in contact by phone or messenger. Battalion orders came from Corps H.Q. to H.Q. and Service Company and then were passed on to the other companies. The unit was split up like this for a month, during which time the men were not allowed to leave the camp. In July 1944 the 553rd moved to a marshalling area in Plymouth from where they sailed to Utah beach as part of Patton's 3rd Army.

While on the continent the 553rd built bridges on the Saar and Moselle Rivers. The latter made it possible for Patton to capture Nancy and move to Metz in September 1944. The unit also used its equipment on the Rhine, South of Koblenz, to replace bridges blown up by the retreating Third Reich. When not building bridges the men of the unit established engineer depots and transported equipment for other groups like the U.S. Navy who needed Landing Crafts (L.C.V.P.) to use on the Rhine.

The 553rd were credited with 4 battle stars: Ardennes-Alsace, Central Europe, Northern France and Rhineland. The unit finally sailed back to the U.S. early in 1946.

Meanwhile, in October 1944 the 408th Field Artillery Battalion, under the command of Colonel E.C. Norman, arrived at Foxley. Tom Glennon, a doctor with the 123rd General Hospital, describes their arrival:

"One morning, about the middle of October 1944, we were awakened to a strange sight in the large assembly area across the street from our Officer's Club. There, lined up in full battle array, were ten large field artillery pieces, Long Toms, as they were affectionately called." - The Officers Club - Thomas Glennon.

The personnel of this group occupied Foxley Manor House and the land around it while training for the battlefields of Europe.

A month later the 408th were joined by the 548th Field Artillery Group, which had left New York on November 1st aboard the Ile de France, a former French passenger liner. John Keller, a sergeant with the 548th, comments on the sea journey:

"Even those who normally enjoy sea travel agree that the best thing about troop transport is 'debarking'." - 548th Battalion from Activation to Victory in Europe.

He describes the messing arrangements aboard the British manned liner as *'a ghastly experience.'*

The 548th Field Artillery Group had been formed on April 13 1944 at Camp Hood, Texas. As Invasion plans were made it was decided that more artillery groups would be needed on the continent than was originally planned for. Lack of time meant that units could not be formed from scratch

Charles Rzeszutko 1944 (C. Rzeszutko).

Dog tag found in Foxley Wood (M. Collins).

Pencil drawing of Hereford from 548th Field Artillery Battalion from Activation to Victory in Europe.

 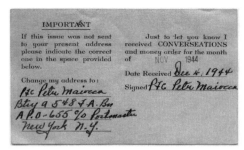

Card sent by Pete Maoicca of the 548th while at Foxley (Author's collection).

so Field Artillery Groups were formed from elements of coastal batteries which, up to this time had been defending the coasts of the U.S. Since Pearl Harbor there had been no further attacks from the Japanese on mainland America so the authorities decided that the well trained artillery men would be best deployed in Europe. The 548th Field Artillery Group was formed from personnel of the 9th, 22nd and 23rd Coast Artillery Regiments. The Commanding Officer was Lieutenant Colonel William F. Kerr.

On November 9 the Ile de France sailed up the Firth of Clyde, dropping anchor at Gouroch, Scotland. On 11 November the men boarded ferries for the short journey to Greenock and then travelled by train to Moorhampton Station where they arrived in typical English weather. As John Keller reports:

"Driving rain and a bumpy truck ride made even the cold bleak looking billets at Camp Foxley look pleasant." - from 548th Battalion from Activation to Victory in Europe.

Sergeant Charles Rzeszutko remembers the mud at the camp made the manoeuvring of artillery and heavy equipment a challenge. While at Foxley Charles spent a week in the hospital nursing a heavy cold. Charles's dog tag was found at Foxley in the 1990's and after extensive searching for his current address it was finally returned to him in 2004.

While at Foxley the men of both Field Artillery Battalions spent the time training to handle the huge guns. Day and night, whatever the weather, the crews went through the routines of loading and firing. Some men were sent to collect trucks and equipment to equip the unit for fighting and some attended service schools at Liverpool and Cardiff. A small detachment of the 548th went on detached service with a combat engineer battalion engaged in bomb damage reconstruction in London. John Keller reports:

2 halves of map showing route of 548th across Europe.
(from 548th Battalion from Activation to Victory in Europe - per C.Rzeszutko).

"*During the few weeks they worked as engineers under daily V-bomb fire this small group of men brought great credit to the battalion and were actually the first of our men to come under fire of the enemy even though the unit did not actually enter combat until February 1945.*" - *548th Battalion from Activation to Victory in Europe.*

Whilst at Foxley the men were allowed passes if they wished to spend time in Hereford, London and other English cities. John recalls:

"*Soldiers and officers who had friends or relatives in England had good opportunity to visit them. England, although ravaged and torn after years of war, still maintained enough liquor and food to make travel enjoyable. American Red Cross facilities in all English cities always made it possible for a soldier to visit and be comfortable. Old England with its traditions and history, cathedrals and castles, was of great interest to the historically minded. The difficulty that arose in becoming accustomed to the shortages due to war, served to show those who had not taken the war seriously enough, that war is hard even on home territory, especially in a country subjected to direct attack from the enemy as England has been for many years. Yank soldiers will never become accustomed to the slow mode of English life, but every nation has its customs and habits and reserve is a manner of the English.*

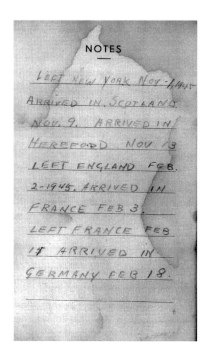

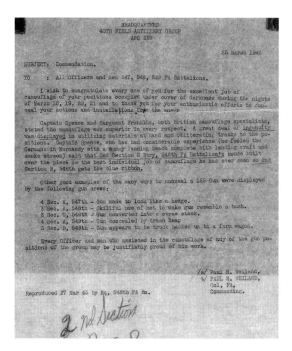

*Left - Notes made by Charles Rzeszutko in 1945. N.B. date on first line
should be 1944 not 1945 (C.Rzeszutko).
Right - Commendation earned by 548th F.A. Battalion (C. Rzeszutko).*

*Visits to bombed out areas in the large cities and the German launched
V-bombs that were landing, daily impressed every soldier that the Germans were
a fanatical and deadly enemy. Every soldier realised that the U.S.A. was very
fortunate in not having its cities subjected to direct warfare as were the cities of
European nations." - From 548th Battalion from Activation to Victory
in Europe.*

In December the 408th left Foxley for France and Germany. On
January 24 1945 Major Bowen, the 548th's Executive Officer left for
London, to work as Liaison Officer in directing the movement of the
Battalion to the Continent. On January 28 Captain Elliot, five other
officers and 25 enlisted men of the 548th left Camp Foxley for the
Continent as Advanced Detail.

The remainder of the 548th prepared the equipment for the long road
journey to Weymouth and short sea voyage to LeHavre, France. On January
31 at 0600 hours the convoy of vehicles set off for marshalling area D14
where they arrived at 2300 hours on the same day. From February 1 to 5 the

units of the battalion were deployed in L.S.T's and shipped to France. They arrived in LeHavre on February 3 and then travelled to Germany arriving on February 18. In Germany the unit received a commendation for its use of camouflage. Charles Rzeszutko's section, B. Battery, received a special mention in the commendation for disguising its piece as a house.

Tom Glennon, back at Foxley recalling good times spent with men of both Field Artillery Groups was saddened:

" *- to learn later that some of those fine young men were lost in action a few short months after leaving Foxley." - The Officer's Club - Thomas Glennon.*

Members of the 548th with their Long Tom (C.Rzeszutko).

Members of the 548th in Europe (C.Rzeszutko).

Chapter 4

12TH U.S. HOSPITAL CENTER

During the early stages of the war in Europe E.T.O. Chief Surgeon General Paul R. Hawley calculated that 90,000 hospital beds would be required to cater for American casualties from Operation Overlord and the campaign in Europe. American forces did requisition a small number of established British hospitals, but most were already set aside for the use of British troops. A number of owners of English country houses offered their homes to be used as hospitals for the American forces but few were suitable. It became necessary for the American government to plan a building programme for 116 hospitals, this figure to include 36 station hospitals and 16 general hospitals. Suitable hospital sites would need to be adjacent to water, gas and sewerage facilities with easy accessibility to roads and railways.

Hawley required the hospitals to be in clusters of four or five for greater efficiency. Each cluster would be known as a Hospital Center. The Hospital Center would be a group of hospitals, general, station and convalescent, operating under a single headquarters. Station hospitals would serve the needs of troops training in the U.K. while General hospitals would take patients wounded in combat on the Continent, General Hospitals having the capacity of just over one thousand beds, while Station Hospitals could take just over 800 patients. Convalescent hospitals would take convalescing patients from both types of hospital.

Hawley intended patients being evacuated from the Continent to travel by train. Each train would carry two to three hundred patients. As patients arrived at the Hospital Center they could be directed to the hospital which would best deal with their injuries. Thus each hospital within a group could concentrate on a certain type of surgery or treatment.

There were to be seven Hospital Centers in the U.K. These would be situated in Taunton, Somerset; Blandford, Dorset; Devizes, Wiltshire; Cirencester, Gloucestershire; Whitchurch, Shropshire; Newmarket, Cambridgeshire and Great Malvern, Worcestershire. The 12th Hospital

Center at Great Malvern was one of the largest centers. As well as American patients it was responsible for the welfare of a large number of French patients. The mission of the 12th Hospital Center was to:

" - act as a Headquarters for a group of from three to ten general hospitals. Within the scope of this function was included the training of personnel in administrative, supply and professional procedures, whereby attached hospitals could be relieved of administrative and supply details and problems by coordinating their activities, thus attention might be devoted to the improvement of professional services." - 12th Hospital Center Archives.

The 12th Medical Hospital Center had been activated in 1942 at Camp Gruber, Oklahoma and sailed for England on the U.S.A.T. Cristobal in a convoy of about thirty ships. On 9th

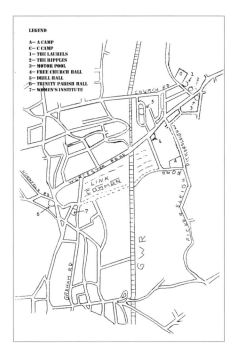

Map of buildings used at Malvern Link.

March the ship docked at Swansea, Glamorganshire and the personnel disembarked and entrained for Great Malvern. On 11th March the 12th set up the Hospital Center at Malvern Link, Worcestershire. Various prominent buildings around the town were commandeered for use as headquarters and living quarters.

On 20th April the Commanding Officer, Colonel Asa M. Lehman, received a telephone call from the Surgeon General, Western Base Section, to inform him that the Center would be opened on 22nd April and this was substantiated by a letter, dated 22nd April and received 26th April, to that effect. The Hospital Centre at Great Malvern began operating as a headquarters for the 19th, 53rd, 55th, 90th and 96th General Hospitals from that date. However, there was some discrepancy over the opening date as on 3 June a letter was received from Headquarters, Western Base Section, dated 30 May stating that the 12th Medical Hospital Center was officially opened as of 0001 hours 8 May 1944. The difference of a fortnight in the paperwork did not affect the smooth running of the setting up of the Hospital Center. On 23 June and 30 July the 99th and 123rd General

Hospitals respectively at Foxley Camp, Herefordshire were attached to the 12th Hospital Center. By September 1944 the Center had nineteen hospitals under its administration.

Plant Number	Place	Number of hospital
4167	Stoneleigh	307 S.H.
4168	Bromsgrove	123 S.H.
4169	Wolverley	52 G.H.
4170	Bewdley	297 G.H.
4171	Bewdley	114 G.H.
4172	Blackmore Park	93 G.H.
4173	Blackmore Park	155 G.H.
4174	Malvern Wells	96 G.H.
4175	Malvern Wells	53 G.H.
4176	Malvern Wells	55 G.H.
4177	Leominster	135 G.H.
4178	Foxley	123 G.H.
4179	Foxley	156 G.H.
4180	Kington	122 G.H.
4181	Kington	107 G.H.
4182	Abergavenny	279 S.H.
4183	Rhyd Lafar	81 G.H.
4148	Camarthen	232 S.H.

S.H.- Station Hospital. G.H. - General Hospital.

On 10 June 1944 the first trainload of casualties from Normandy intended for the 12th Hospital Center was unloaded at Malvern Wells Station:

"some difficulty was encountered in the unloading of these casualties due to the inexpedient condition and arrangement of the station platform and adjacent features. This situation had been anticipated early in April 1944 when a survey was made by the Center Commanding Officer. On 29 April 1944 an urgent request was made for the construction and improvements o facilities for the loading and unloading of patients at the Malvern Wells Railroad Station. However progression of this project was delayed and the construction of a new siding was not completed and available for use until 26 June 1944 when it was first used for the unloading of patients." - 12th Hospital Center Archives.

As well as the railway the Hospital Center had the use of a nearby airfield but:

" - *allotments for our evacuation of patients to the Zone of Interior often resulted in much confusion and delay.*" - *12th Hospital Center Archives.*

This was due to problems connected with weather conditions which led to delays in plane schedules. Sometimes patients would arrive at the airfield to find that planes had been grounded. This would often result in patients having to be transported to and from the airfield several times before the plane actually took off.

INDIVIDUAL HOSPITAL STATUS   REAKDOWN
31 December 1944

	TOTAL BEDS NORMAL	TOTAL BEDS (EXP)	TOTAL BEDS ACTUAL	PNTS AWAIT-ING EVAC	TOTAL PNTS IN HOSP	VAC BEDS MED	VAC BEDS SURG	VAC BEDS MENTAL CLOSED	VAC BEDS MENTAL OPEN	TOTAL VACANT BEDS
52GH:	1084	450	1534	22	1346	72	114	0	2	188
53GH:	1082	435	1517	720	1467	25	25	0	0	50
55GH:	1082	435	1517	354	1396	30	65	0	26	121
81GH:	834	330	1164	13	823	121	199	2	19	341
93GH:	1084	375	1459	774	1272	95	92	0	0	187
96GH:	1082	345	1427	250	1310	5	0	96	16	117
107GH:	1000	442	1442	17	1361	15	66	0	0	81
114GH:	1000	442	1442	5	1368	7	27	0	40	74
122GH:	1000	442	1442	27	1313	121	8	0	0	129
123GH:	1000	442	1442	55	1294	52	96	0	0	148
135GH:	834	330	1164	9m	1017	82	60	2	3	147
155GH:	1082	285	1367	228	1008	104	255	0	0	359
156GH:	1000	442	1442	11	1133	160	104	25	20	309
297GH:	1000	442	1442	85	1158	72	211	0	1	284
825CC:	2500	420	2920	1	2719	201	0	0	0	201
833CC:	400	0	400	0	392	0	8	0	0	8

(Cont)

	TOTAL BEDS NORMAL	TOTAL BEDS (EXP)	TOTAL BEDS ACTUAL	PNTS AWAIT-ING EVAC	TOTAL PNTS IN HOSP	VAC BEDS MED	VAC BEDS SURG	VAC BEDS MENTAL CLOSED	VAC BEDS MENTAL OPEN	TOTAL VACANT BEDS
232SH:	750	330	1080	0	1037	16	7	0	20	43
279SH:	834	300	1134	18	820	81	197	2	34	314
826CC:	1084	2591	3675	0	3633	36	6	0	0	42
TOTAL:	19732	9278	29010	2589	25867	1295	1540	127	181	3143

Data for 12th Hospital Center December 1944.

In October 1944 the organisation of the Hospital Centers was revised. On 2 October orders were issued by H.Q. U.K. Base announcing the establishment of seven provisional Hospital Groups in the U.K. One of these groups, the 5th Hospital Group, was to be established with headquarters in the vicinity of Great Malvern. The Commanding Officer of the new unit was to be Colonel Lehman. On 13 October orders were sent from Headquarters, U.K. Base which attached the 12th Medical Hospital Center and its assigned units to the 5th Hospital Group.

The 12th Hospital Center became the subject of several magazine articles. Robert Littell, freelance journalist for the Readers Digest described the Hospital Center in the following article entitled:

"HOW OUR WOUNDED CAME BACK FROM NORMANDY

At evening the wounded reached the final link in the chain of their healing, at least in England. Here, in rolling open country, dozens of Nissen huts look out upon distant sheep and stone walls. This is one of half a dozen general hospitals in the area. Together they form a center where the highest medical skill is assembled from great universities and hospitals. Here specialists give each man's particular wound care that would be hard to equal in any civilian hospital.

I agree with the colonel in the medical corps who said: 'The wounded G.I. is getting a much better break than the average citizen who is hit by a car in the United States." - Readers Digest September 1944.

The Temple Telegram, a Texas newspaper, also describes the 12th Hospital Center:

"wounded fighters from France are routed within a few hours to a cluster of completely equipped hospitals in England by a United States Army Medical Center which is a key unit in the medical services smoothly moving transmission belt from the liberation front.

One of a small number of such centers organised by the Army, the unit is headed by Colonel Asa M. Lehman of Ardmore, Pennsylvania, a veteran hospital Commander with 28 years of regular army experience in two wars. Under Colonel Lehman's direction the center controls thousands of hospital beds and a large pool of ambulances available to rush patients to hospitals with plenty of bed space.

The center can handle the arrival of several hospital trains at the same time, and the huge hospitals can absorb many trainloads without having to evacuate patients to other areas. But the organisation of the hospital system is designed to keep patients who have recovered from battle injuries or illnesses moving along to convalescent camps or back to military duty.

Incoming wounded men, who have already received preliminary treatment from field stations, and first aid soldiers are carefully sorted out for assignment to particular hospitals. Those with chest injuries are sent to hospital which may also treat other types of cases but concentrates on chest wounds, burned men and men requiring plastic surgery go to another hospital, and patients requiring operations on the nerves go to still another one.

Highly specialized physicians and surgeons, experts in their fields, are shifted quickly and freely from one hospital to another for casework, diagnoses and consultations. Transfer of a physician from one hospital to another, which may be short a top notch man in some phases of medicine, is facilitated by the medical center which attempts to eliminate as much red tape as is possible.

All patients scheduled to be evacuated from the hospitals to other areas are assembled at one hospital. The hospital most conveniently located in relation to railroad stations and airfields is selected for this purpose. The medical center maintains a teleprinter connected to the Headquarters at the European Theater of Operations, trunk telephones, and a switchboard connecting all the hospitals in the cluster attached to the center.

When men are ready for transfer back to their outfits, to convalescent camps, or rest centers in the United States, the center prepares their orders and checks their records to make sure that all necessary information on their medical and military background goes with them.

Under the supervision of Colonel Lehman a special train siding has been built at the railroad station in the small English city (Great Malvern) where the medical center is located. The center plans to have a hospital train on hand at all times, if possible, and to use the siding as a base for the operation and unloading of the train."
- Temple Telegram 2.07.44.

Chapter 5
99TH GENERAL HOSPITAL

At the beginning of 1944 Higgs and Hill, a London based contractor, moved on to the site at Foxley to construct two purpose built hospitals. Building materials were transported by train to Moorhampton Station and then by truck to the camp. The land around the Manor House that had been beautifully landscaped by Sir Urevale Price in 1743 had now become divided by concrete roadways.

On June 5 1944 the 99th General Hospital, which was to come within the jurisdiction of the 12th Hospital Center, proceeded to Foxley to inhabit the new hospital plant. The 99th had been activated at Fort Andrews, Massachusetts, on 25 June 1943 and sailed to Liverpool on the H.M.T. Rangitiki on 5 April 1944. The hospital personnel disembarked from 19 to 20 April and then travelled by rail to a medical staging area at Llandudno in North Wales. From Llandudno the 99th were directed to Foxley.

One nurse remembers her arrival at Foxley, Hospital Plant 4178:

"On 5th June 1944 a song drifted out of an army truck on a rough road at Camp Foxley, England. The figures were hidden by army gray-green uniforms, but the voices were feminine.

The camp was situated in a beautiful valley about 10 miles from the nearest town. It was a dual-purpose camp and the 99th General Hospital was assigned to Camp B. Everyone assisted in cleaning of the installations. It was necessary to do a great deal of improvising. One requirement was to make each ward identical. It meant salvaging everything available from glass containers to pieces of bunker. Desks were mess tables. The stoves smoked, everyone had to learn how to fire them. Two big problems were presented. The first was how to get food to the wards and served hot to the patient. The problem was solved by filling the carts with boiling water and taking them directly to the wards. Trays and dishes were kept in warming ovens and food was served immediately on arrival. The second problem was the pitch mastic floors. Every footprint left a mark. This was a housekeeping challenge to every nurse and ward man. The floors were waxed and by continual polishing were left in good condition." - 99th General Hospital Archives.

The personnel attached to the 99th had to work quickly to prepare the hospital buildings for receiving patients. A detail of nurses and enlisted men were put to work in the operating rooms, which were in a separate building near the centre of the hospital. It was necessary to shovel mud and plaster out of the room and use a large quantity of soap and water to make the room ready for patients. Water had to be carried in buckets from the powerhouse a few feet away. It took five days to make the operating room ready for use.

A central supply room was set up in another building, separate from the rest of the buildings but easily reached by all wards and the operating theatre. Cupboards and shelves were built to create storage space. Autoclaves and sterilisers were installed and instruments were unstacked, washed and arrayed in cabinets. A sewing machine was put into operation making all types of dressings and wrappers and cases for sterile goods. Cultures were taken from all cans, jars and solutions to ensure that the contents were sterile.

A laboratory was set up in a single storey building of temporary construction and it was soon well equipped with material and supplies. A shock laboratory was set up in the shock ward and was prepared with copper sulfate studies for shock and plasma loss, blood typing and cross matching.

The chief of the Roetgenological service and ten enlisted men prepared an X-ray department in one of the buildings. This section was ready for operation when the first patients arrived at the hospital. Seven weeks later it had carried out X-rays of 1408 patients.

The nurses were quartered on the side of the hill overlooking the rest of the hospital area. There were eight nurses to a hut and one was set-aside for the night nurses, giving them a quiet place to sleep. The huts were constructed of Maycrete (sand, cement and sawdust) and measured 60 x 18.5 feet. They had plain glass windows and a front and rear door. The pitched roof was made of corrugated asbestos and had small chimneys protruding from it.

On 12 June the hospital was officially open to receive patients and on the 16th the first 127 battle casualties arrived by train at Moorhampton Station. The patients were predominantly battle casualties who had been evacuated from France and for the most part had already had some treatment at a forward General Hospital. The official records of the 99th for June state:

"Hospital Trains began arriving. Each train-load was received in a more expectatious manner than the last. The hospital was soon operating to capacity." - 99th General Hospital Archives.

*Hospital Train at Moorhampton Station. Orderlies unloading patients.
Photo per William H. Smith.*

Moorhampton Station - pre-war (M. Powell).

Moorhampton Station - disused 2003 (M. Collins).

The personnel found that a number of battle casualties required skin grafts. The Surgical Service was able to carry out this delicate operation using leucocytic cream, which was prepared in the laboratory at the hospital. Many patients also needed blood transfusions and while no blood bank was maintained, a high percentage of officers and enlisted men were on the volunteer donor list.

The hospital began its work with a staff of 53 officers, 83 nurses, two warrant officers, two Physical Therapy Aides and 496 enlisted men. By June 19 the full quota of 56 commissioned officers and 496 enlisted men was achieved. An American Red Cross Unit was also attached to the hospital. The records state that:

"The purpose of this unit was to furnish volunteer aid to the sick and wounded and to act in matters of voluntary relief in accordance with military authority and as a medium of communication between the people of the United States and the men in the Armed Forces." - 99th General Hospital Archives.

The primary function of the American Red Cross when attached to a hospital was to provide welfare and recreational activities for patients and social service to able-bodied members of the Medical Detachment.

Specifically the official archives list eight phases that the American Red Cross unit attached to the 99th General Hospital were involved in:

1. *Obtaining health and welfare reports. These include communications from Home Service Chapters requesting information about patients and personnel of the Medical Detachment and requests for information on families back home.*
2. *General casework concerning family, personal and medical problems.*
3. *Making loans on an emergency basis to cover personal and incidental expenses.*
4. *Issuance on an emergency basis of cigarettes, candy, toilet articles and so forth.*
5. *Establishing a Red Cross recreation hall where patients come for relaxation and diversion from ward routine.*
6. *Special events such as Bingo Parties, Carnivals and parties for occasions such as Hallowe'en and Christmas.*
7. *A craft program, which combines the use of new and salvaged materials.*
8. *Distribution of books and magazines turned over to Red Cross by Special Service. - 99th General Hospital Archives.*

Normally five Red Cross workers would make up one unit but due to a shortage of overseas Red Cross Personnel there were only four attached to the 99th. The Assistant Field Director, Miss Ruth E. Holland, had responsibility for administration and social service, there was a recreation worker who planned and presented recreational programmes, a staff aide who assisted the recreation worker and a secretary who also acted as a hostess in the Red Cross rooms.

It soon became obvious that it would be necessary to employ British citizens to help run the hospital efficiently. From the beginning a maintenance crew of 12 men and 30 other civilians was required. The archivist for the 99th states:

"From the time that we arrived in Foxley until July 25th civilians were employed as quickly as they could be obtained so that on the latter date we had two complete maintenance crews, four switchboard operators, three seamstresses, one stenographer and four laborers." - 99th General Hospital Archives.

The civilians were paid through the British Pay and Establishment Office in Birmingham, which mailed them their weekly payroll checks. The British employees mainly performed clerical and utility work but were not permitted to view classified material.

Edward Spencer was the electrician on one of the maintenance crews. During the school holidays his daughter, Doreen, would accompany him to work, catching the 'Yeomans' bus from Hinton to Mansel Lacy. While her father was working Doreen would visit the injured soldiers, sitting at the foot of their beds to talk to them. She recalls that she was given lots of chocolate and sweets, which made her very popular at school. She also remembers being amazed at the sight of the large cooking tubs with pats of butter floating on the top:

"We did not know what it was to have butter leave alone cook with it."

Left - Edward Spencer, electrician at Foxley (D.Skinner).
Right - Doreen Spencer, daughter of Edward, at Foxley (D.Skinner).

Horace (known as Joe) Bradbury, who lived at Norton Canon, was the water engineer at the site. He often took his twin daughters, Jennifer and Susan, to visit the hospital. Susan remembers the camp as:

"an enormous expanse of concrete and buildings, somehow mysterious and exciting."

She clearly remembers the operating theatre with its large table and lights above it:

"My lasting impression, as a youngster, was one of horror."

Some of the patients at the hospital visited the Bradburys in their home, sometimes bringing silk stockings for Doris, Horace's wife. Susan reminisces:

"What really sticks in my mind is that they brought chocolate and bananas, the first time I can recall eating either. I know my sister and I were fascinated by 'having to take the coats off the bananas.' My other memory is that one of the Americans would not eat fruitcake because he didn't like the 'plums'. My sister would refuse to eat fruit cake for years afterwards."

The water for the site came from the River Wye at Byford, about 5 1/2 miles south east of Foxley. The pumping station was located at Byford and had the capacity of approximately 20,000 gallons per hour. Here the water was filtered and treated with alum. Following filtration ammonia chloride and sodium carbonate were added. Horace worked between the two sites: at Byford and Foxley. There were some problems with the water supply. Occasionally the engineers were unable to operate the plant for a time. At other times the number of patients at the hospital increased beyond the anticipated number and it was necessary to conserve the water for short periods.

While the 99th were at Foxley every aspect of the patients' and staff's health was covered. A dental clinic was set up and during the seven weeks of their stay the Dental Services, led by Lieutenant Colonel Edgar J. Jacques rendered 1169 examinations, 2143 sittings, 512 fillings, 88 prosthetic casts, 67 teeth extracted, 2 fractured jaws treated, 8 Stomatitus Vincents treated, 193 oral prophylactics and 99 X-ray exposures.

Jennifer and Susan Bradbury at Foxley (S. Williams).

From 12 to 27 June there was also a Venereal disease Control Programme, which was set up by the Venereal Disease Control Officer, Captain Herman Kline. This consisted of:

1. *Lectures on aspects of Venereal Diseases, their control and prevention.*
2. *The foundation of small V.D. control groups headed by an N.C.O. whose duty it was to instruct men in V.D. prophylaxis.*
3. *Operation of a prophylaxis station in the Unit dispensary.*
4. *Establishment and operation of prophylaxis station in the city of Hereford from 1st to 24th July* (This came under the jurisdiction of the 156th General Hospital when the 99th left Foxley.)
5. *All men returning from pass were examined to determine if they were under the influence of an intoxicant. If they were they were given a prophylaxis. - 99th General Hospital Archives.*

```
                    99TH GENERAL HOSPITAL              MGM/bw
                     WBS  SOS  ETOUSA
                   APO 115, U. S. Army


        PROGRAM FOR ANNIVERSARY DAY--25 June 1944

        No Reville

 0900  - Address-Lt. Colonel Henry S. Murphey.

 0915  - History of the Organization-Major Milo G. Meyer.

 0930  - Introduction of Officers Activating Unit and Original
         Cadre-Lt. Col. Edgar J. Jacques.

 1030  - Protestant Services in the Chapel

 1115  - Catholic Mass in the Chapel

 1330  - I. D. R. Platoon Competition.

 1415  - Track Meet:

              EM              NURSES            OFFICERS

         100 yd dash      Potato Race          Sack Race
         880 yd dash
         High-jump
         Shot Put
         Broad Jump
         Relay Race (4 men ea platoon)
         Football Throw
         Baseball Throw for accuracy

 1630  - Supper out of doors---Barbecue if possible.

 1900  - Baseball Game Between the Officers and 1st 4 Grades.

         AREA:  Rear of Camp #2--Ball Diamond and Field.

         Adequate care of Patients and Hospital equipment will be
 maintained.

         A compilation of points from the track meet and I. D. R.
 will be made.  Platoon accumulating most points will be awarded
 a suitable prize.

              For the Commanding Officer:

                                      M. G. MEYER
                                      Major  MC
                                      Executive Officer

                         - 1 -
```

Programme for Anniversary celebrations (99th General Hospital Archives).

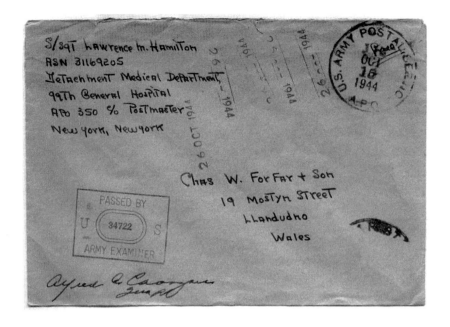

Cover sent by Staff Sergeant Lawrence M. Hamilton,
99th General Hospital (Author's collection).

On June 25 1944 the unit celebrated its first anniversary with a church service and a track meet. As many as could attended the celebrations although a skeleton staff was maintained on the wards.

On 25 July 1944 Hospital Plant No. 4178, site number one was officially entrusted to the 156th General Hospital. One nurse sums up her feelings as she left Foxley:

"The hospital was in operation for seven weeks when the unit was told it was to go to France. - this was the first time that the personnel had worked together as a unit and it was like giving up something that had become apart of them. Everyone left Foxley with fond memories, rich experiences and an eagerness to get started on another assignment nearer to the front." - 99th General Hospital Archives.

On 28 July the unit departed by train from Moorhampton station to Llandudno. By the 29th all of the personnel had returned to Llandudno for staging prior to movement to the Continent. On 18 August the personnel sailed on the U.S.S. William Pepperell and the H.M.T. City of Canterbury for Utah Beach, to live in France under field conditions until 17 September.

Chapter 6

156TH GENERAL HOSPITAL

The 156th General Hospital was activated December 23 1943. The hospital was stationed at Camp McCoy, Wisconsin until 10 June 1944 when it left for Camp Kilmer, New Jersey for overseas processing. On June 22 the unit left New York aboard the Queen Elizabeth and sailed to Glasgow. From Glasgow the 156th travelled by train to Camp Foxley where it occupied Site 2 (Hospital Plant 4179) from 28 June until 25 July 1945.

On arrival in England the Transportation Department, consisting of 27 men, received 25 vehicles: one British Sedan, one Jeep, one Weapons Carrier, four Command Cars, eight ambulances (six American, two British), one Cargo Truck, one Dump Truck, two 1 1/2 ton trucks, three 2 1/2 ton Cargo Trucks and three trailers. The Transportation Department was responsible for transporting patients to and from the 156th General Hospital and also for furnishing transport for other hospitals in the 12th Hospital Center. Two hours per week training in the maintenance and operation of the vehicles was provided. Because of the fuel shortage in England it was necessary to try and consolidate trips whenever necessary.

When the 156th arrived at Foxley Site 2 was still in the process of completion. The enlisted men were billeted in barracks, which housed 28 men in double deck bunks. Lieutenant Colonel Sullivan, the Executive Officer, reported that the housing was 'adequate' although:

"Austerity scales for living accommodations are not grossly exceeded. - Soon after arrival in this theater it was found that buildings of the type used there were not of sturdy construction and were in constant need of repair." - 156th General Hospital Archives.

Patients were expected any day so the Medical Supply Department began to uncrate and issue supplies to the various wards and departments immediately. When the 99th General Hospital vacated Site 1 (Hospital Plant 4178) the 156th moved to the completed site and took over the care of the 1087 patients already on site. Lieutenant Colonel Sullivan commented that this move:

" *- brought out the strengths and weaknesses of the nursing staff." - 156th General Hospital Archives.*

With the exception of approximately ten nurses all were experienced in army routine, having joined the 156th shortly after the completion of their basic training. Unfortunately none of the nurses had ever experienced the arrival of a convoy of wounded patients and they were not prepared for the situation that they found themselves in at Foxley. Lieutenant Colonel Sullivan reports:

"It would seem that some basic training for overseas nursing would have been invaluable with emphasis being placed on standardization and its value." - 156th General Hospital Archives.

There was a lack of specialty nurses among the 156th, particularly those trained in operating procedures. On the positive side it was noted that:

"Even though many of the nurses were young and inexperienced they were always willing to do more than their share and give unstintingly of their off duty time. This is particularly true of nurses helping to entertain bed and ambulatory patients. Since there was a definite lack of space for relaxation of ambulatory patients the nurses helped to alleviate this situation by planning many unique and entertaining ward parties." - 156th General Hospital Archives.

Unfortunately on the transfer of the 156th to Site 1 a number of problems occurred. It was soon discovered that memorandum receipts did not accurately show the location of all of the property that had already been distributed on Site 2. To take care of this situation a complete inventory of the hospital was made and the property reallocated. According to the archives of the 156th the Supply Department was '*constantly challenged*' during their time at Foxley. Lieutenant Colonel Sullivan remarks that:

"It was necessary to exercise considerable ingenuity in operating a Supply Office in the United Kingdom. Constant improvisation was the order of the day. Articles, otherwise unobtainable, frequently were purchased through the British. The clothing situation for the patients has been very tight. No patient was detained in the hospital because clothing could not be obtained but supplies on various occasions were so close as to cause some anxiety." - 156th General Hospital Archives.

When the first convoy of patients arrived at the hospital it was necessary to borrow blankets and litters from neighbouring hospitals.

The 156th also found the messing arrangements on Site 1 to be unsatisfactory. Three Mess Halls were operated at the hospital, one for the patients, one for the enlisted men and one for officers. The approaches to the Mess Halls took the form of covered walkways with roofs but no sides. This meant that patients were exposed to the elements while queuing for food.

Covered walkways at the 53rd General Hospital in Malvern showing how
patients would have very little shelter from the elements.
These were of the sort to be seen at Foxley (Malvern Library).

The messing equipment was also found to be lacking. Lieutenant Colonel
Sullivan reports:

Most of the equipment is of British make. On the whole it has proven
unsatisfactory. - The location of equipment was on our arrival unsatisfactory, not
conducive to efficiency. - Worn out equipment is difficult to replace and at present
there are several items on back order." - 156th General Hospital Archives.

The Messing Staff encountered problems with the stoves, food carts
and refrigerators:

"The stoves are made with too small a firebox so that the amount of heat
obtained from them is either inadequate for the proper cooking of food or so delays
the preparation of food that the mess hours are retarded with consequent inefficiency
and confusion." - 156th General Hospital Archives.

The fuel for the stoves was found to be of poor quality and the stove space
was considerably below that needed to properly serve the number of patients.
Electrical heating units in warming ovens on the wards were found to be
inefficient for the job they were designed for and difficult to repair. The water
warmed food carts also came in for criticism.

"The food carts provided for carrying food to bed patients are of poor
construction and furthermore are supplied with metal wheels. This combination of
structural deficiencies, particularly when associated with corrugated cement walk,s
leads to frequent breakdowns, which at times results in spilling of these carts and
wastage of critical food. The lining enamel of these containers in the carts wears off
readily and cannot be replaced. Rust supervenes and an insanitary food container
results." - 156th General Hospital Archives.

The size of the refrigerators was found to be too small for the storage of the
food provided, so in warm weather food was spoilt on a number of occasions.

The British built grease traps also came in for criticism and the Americans found the local contractors who were responsible for garbage disposal, unreliable. This led to a problem with rats and it was necessary to institute a rat control programme immediately. Mechanical traps were periodically set around the food disposal depots. By the end of the year this problem, at least, was under control.

The 156th found that the food rations provided for the camp were:

" - *adequate, but at no time excessive.*" - *156th General Hospital Archives.*

The fresh vegetables in particular, came in for criticism:

"*On several occasions they were found on arrival to be in such poor condition that by the time they were cleaned the issue was found to be inadequate in amount.*" - *156th General Hospital Archives.*

It was necessary for the 156th to surmount these problems quickly as approximately 5,500 meals had to be served daily, of which 3,900 were for patients. It was also necessary to produce 25 to 50 special diets consisting largely of soft, low residue and low fat types. Some patients had to be fed hourly.

Within a week of the 156th assuming control of Site 1 over 250 more patients arrived. From then on convoys averaging 300 patients each arrived every eight to ten days. A large percentage of these casualties had been injured in the St. Lo drive. It was necessary for the Surgical Department to borrow ten officers from the Medical Department to help cope with the large number of casualties. It also had to rapidly adapt itself to the technique of secondary closure of wounds, which it was unfamiliar with. Another problem that the Surgical Department encountered was that patients were spending too long at the hospital and -

" - *minor wounds resulted in as long periods of disability as some major wounds.*" - *156th General Hospital Archives.*

To counteract this, the department encouraged active exercises while patients were still bedridden and the transfer of patients to rehabilitation wards as soon as possible. The Rehabilitation Service was responsible for preparing the patients for return to their units. The personnel of this department found that:

"*early transfer of patients from general to rehabilitation wards and - the establishment of a program sufficiently full and varied so as to keep the patients well occupied but not bored.*" - *156th General Hospital Archives.*

was the key to the success of the department. They also found that the psychological factor of donning a uniform to replace pyjamas on the rehabilitation wards improved the patient's recovery. The original allocation of 145 beds to this section was soon found to be insufficient and was gradually increased to 311. It was also necessary to increase the number of staff in the department.

As well as the general programme of exercise for patients in the rehabilitation barracks there was a programme for patients confined to wards. This consisted of:

" - *a daily period of calisthenics under the ward master supervised by the rehabilitation officer and physiotherapist, and a regular period of group discussion held by a convalescent patient officer and frequent training films or stripfilms and lectures." - 156th General Hospital Archives.*

The Physiotherapy Department was responsible for organising and supervising the daily exercises in the wards and also, in cooperation with the orthopedics section, the establishment of remedial exercises for fracture cases amongst the bed and ambulatory patients. However the Physiotherapy Department found the allotted space for the operation of the department to be inadequate. The clinic consisted of just one room. Privacy for ultra-violet treatments and female patients was non-existent. However the enlisted men from this department were very ingenious in the manufacture of exercise equipment. Amongst other items they made a shoulder wheel, Knavel Table and four foot exercisers.

The X-Ray Department also found their allotted space too confined and this resulted:

" - *not only in hampering the efficiency of this department but also in unduly exposing the personnel to X-ray radiation." - 156th General Hospital Archives.*

By the end of 1944 the patients received by the hospital were generally in better condition than those received at the opening of the hospital. This was due to the fact that they were held longer on the Continent in the field hospitals, arriving at Foxley two or three weeks after being wounded, rather than five to ten days:

"One convoy formed rather a disquieting exception. Upon arrival it seemed no different from previous convoys but when, within 48 hours more transfusions were given to patients in this convoy than during the eight months the hospital had been in existence it was apparent that it was different. The difference lay in the fact that nearly all the soldiers had been wounded within five to seven days, They had been in the process of evacuation constantly since the hour they were hit, having never stopped at one place long enough to obtain adequate food and rest. The first morning's operative list produced a startling number of cases of shock. Infected wounds were common. Nearly a week's rest was necessary before operative procedures were resumed". - 156th General Hospital Archives.

Within the 12th Hospital Center each hospital had expertise in several fields. The 156th was designated a 'hand center'. Patients needing treatments on hands were referred to the 156th from other hospitals in the 12th Hospital Center. Captain Frederick D. Troutman of the 156th devised a piece of apparatus, which was found to be extremely valuable in the rehabilitation of injured hands.

The 156th was also designated for the study and treatment of female personnel. A nurses ward for the hospitalisation of sick nurses from Foxley and other nearby general hospitals was operated successfully. The 156th was also a center for the care and disposition of psychotic patients.

The fourth area of expertise for the 156th was the study and treatment of obscure gastrointestinal diseases. The Chief of Medical Service was an experienced gastroscapist both in civilian and army life. Patients needing treatment for gastrointestinal complaints were referred to the 156th from all sections of the United Kingdom. 88 patients were examined at this hospital and all examinations of the stomach were carried out satisfactorily.

Some extensive scientific work was carried out at the 156th concerning the feeding of over 100 malnourished soldiers. All had lost between 15 and 75 pounds in weight and were suffering from various degrees of fatigue, lack of sense of well being and malaise.

"It was our conception that the nutritional element of these illnesses was of paramount importance. Accordingly a plan was conceived whereby ingestion of food in excess of 5000 calories per day derived from 150-250 grams of protein, 600-800 grams of carbohydrate and 150-280 grams of fat was fed by oral route to each patient. To achieve this goal the three regular meals were fed under the supervision of a specially trained dietary staff, supplemented by hourly feedings from 0800 hours to 2100 hours of readily available regular issue food. The net result of this regime was that the average rate of gain of 14.5 pounds in 30 days average hospitality. It is important to realize that this gain in weight in the face of an act of febrile state spared a further depletion of body tissues and instilled into each patient a sense of well being and a desire to return to full duty." - 156th General Hospital Archives.

The 156th also became expert at making acrylic eye prosthesis. On 10 October 1944 the prosthetic subsection of the Dental Section turned its hand to making false eyes as well as false teeth. A new technique for taking impressions of eye sockets for artificial eyes was developed in this department:

"This embodied the use of an acrylic syringe which enabled the impression material to be inserted under the lids. The net result of this improvement was shown in better fitting prostheses and less time consumption in making each eye." - 156th General Hospital Archives.

While at Foxley training programmes for the staff were devised. This generally consisted of eight hours weekly instruction in military knowledge and also on developing proficiency and initiative in the routine administrative and professional duties of the personnel.

"Each week the enlisted men had two hours of departmental training, this was conducted on the wards by ward officers and ward masters. It involved subjects that were pertinent to the moment. For those enlisted men that did not work on the wards departmental training was carried out that was peculiar to their field of endeavor. In addition three hours per week were devoted to lectures on military subjects, lectures regarding articles of war as well as rules of censorship and conduct in the E.T.O. Several hours per week were devoted to mass athletics." - 156th General Hospital Archives.

The training programme for officers was also very thorough. The male officers and nurses had to attend a weekly clinical pathological conference. Each week one of the officers would present a paper of a formal scientific nature. Afterwards there would be discussion. As Lieutenant Colonel Sullivan writes:

"Outside observers have commented that these meetings were highly informative and the best that they had experienced in military medicine." - 156th General Hospital Archives.

The male officers would also be expected to attend an informal 'round table discussion' by the medical staff on any pertinent problems that had arisen. Two hours per week would be devoted by the surgical staff to the review and discussion of anatomical and surgical matters. Each week the medical staff held a one hour meeting on a review of physiology. Mass athletics were also held for a period each week, this would mainly take the form of a volleyball or softball match. The 156th had a softball team in the Hospital Center League and most of the hospital personnel were involved in a softball programme at the site.

As well as the clinical pathological Conference and mass athletics the nurses would be expected to attend a weekly meeting with the Chief Nurse regarding administrative matters and ward management. There would also be a departmental training programme for nurses to attend.

The Special Service Officer at the 156th was responsible for organising a recreational programme for the patients and staff. Movies were shown on each ward at some time during the week. They were also shown to the staff at the hospital (separate showings for officers and enlisted men) three times per week. However there were complaints that films were repeated and that they were sometimes of a 'Class B' nature. Each month two

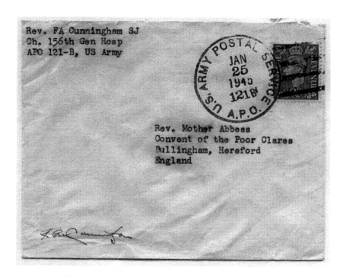

Letter sent by chaplain of 156th General Hospital
to Convent in Hereford (Author's Collection).

U.S.O. shows were presented and dances for the enlisted men and officers were held regularly. The 156th also had an officer's club and a '156 Club' for enlisted men. The personnel of the 156th spent some of their off duty time improving the grounds around the hospital. As the commanding officer Colonel Patton reports in July 1945:

"The general appearance of the hospital grounds in a period of ten months has constantly improved. This was achieved mainly through the enthusiasm and cooperation of the detachment officers and nurses." - 156th General Hospital Archives.

Provision was also made for the religious development of the patients and staff. The 156th had two chaplains, one Protestant and one Catholic. On Sunday there were four Protestant services and two Catholic Masses. There was also a daily Protestant prayer meeting and a daily Catholic Mass. Around ten people attended the Jewish services held every Friday night. The Jewish holy days were celebrated in Hereford where there was a rabbi.

During 1945 several doctors and nurses from the 156th were sent to the Continent for duty in medical units nearer the front. Because of the large numbers of wounded in the battles on the Continent some enlisted men from the hospital were detached from duty with the hospital and retrained for infantry duty. At the end of May 1945 the complete hospital unit was issued with orders to redeploy to the Pacific Theatre of Operations.

On 21 May 1945 the organisation received a verbal order to close the professional services and transfer the remaining patients to Hospital Plant 4179, run by the 123rd General Hospital. The unit departed Foxley the following month. Colonel Patton concludes his report of the 156th's stay at Foxley in May 1945:

"It can be seen that the 156th General Hospital has formed a remarkable duty while in this theater of operations. From an untried group of personnel thrust into a difficult setting and suddenly receiving battle casualties and sick soldiers incident to the St.Lo breakthrough we have evolved into a smooth, well knit, highly efficient unit. All personnel have worked hard and contributed unselfishly to this goal. We point with pride to the record of eight deaths in nearly 8,000 patients and only two deaths in the year 1945 (3059 admissions). - As we close this plant it is safe to say it is in good repair and the grounds can best be described as beautiful. There is an abundance of grass, a profusion of flowers and an air of refinement about the grounds that is conducive to the care of the sick." - 156th General Hospital Archives.

Chapter 7

156TH GENERAL HOSPITAL
- AMERICAN RED CROSS

The programme for the recreation of the patients of the 156th was chiefly carried out by the Red Cross Unit attached to the hospital. The 156th applied for a Red Cross Unit to work alongside them in April 1944, while the hospital was still at Camp McCoy, Wisconsin. The group of five girls arrived at Camp McCoy on May 18. The group consisted of: Lucia Irons, Social Worker; Mary McConnel, Staff Aide; Maude Campbell and Dulcy Goetchius, Recreation workers and Katherine Colton, Secretary.

The unit travelled to Foxley with the 156th, first inhabiting nurses quarters on Site 2 and then on Site 1 when the 99th moved out. The girls took on the work of the Red Cross unit that had been attached to the 99th although it had obviously been:

" - understaffed and it did not pretend to have a full program. The patients had been accustomed to a certain amount of social service and a minimum amount of recreation." - 156th General Hospital Red Cross Archives.

When the 156th moved to Site 1 the hospital was already full of patients and the Red Cross found that they had very little time to get organised:

"We attempted to carry on as the other unit had done but we question our efficiency. There were many new patients who required special services and we were unable to get to them as quickly as we wished" - 156th General Hospital Red Cross Archives.

Towards the end of the year the girls found that they could make a more efficient use of their time by greeting each new convoy as it arrived at the hospital, rather than attempting to visit each new patient on the wards.

"We know that the men liked to feel A.R.C. was here and on the job but we found it impossible to visit wards quickly enough and do an adequate job. Hence we decided one or two workers would be stationed at the hospital entrance and there personally give out cigarettes ('Smokes for Yanks' as well as cigarettes from our own supply.) We are now able to visit wards thoroughly without breaking up our routine

since convoys have been so frequent." - *156th General Hospital Red Cross Archives.*

As well as having time management difficulties when the unit moved to Site 1 there were also problems with supplies. The office supplies had been lost in transit although London headquarters was able to provide an emergency supply that would last for a few weeks. The unit was fortunate in that it had 'inherited' a small supply of 'comfort articles' from the Red Cross Unit attached to the 99th. The girls planned to negotiate with the P.X. to purchase more articles to distribute. By the end of July the girls were able to supply the entire initial needs of the patients with the exception of notepaper. In

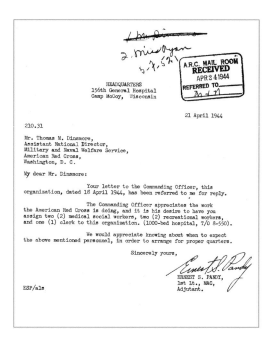

Letter from the 156th General Hospital requesting 5 Red Cross Workers (156th General Hospital Red Cross Archives).

September the supply situation was further complicated when all of the 156th internal supplies were frozen while the Supply Department made an inventory and reorganised all supplies. This situation came as a result of the problems the personnel had in locating all equipment when the hospital moved sites.

Although things were difficult in the first month or so that the unit spent at Foxley, Lucia Irons reported about her staff:

"The workers have been very interested and conscientious about their jobs and their professional attitude in the main is not to be questioned. Each one has a great deal of ability and a good background and much to offer for the Red Cross program." - 156th General Hospital Red Cross Archives.

As soon as the unit was settled on the new site plans were made as to how it would carry out its remit, which was to handle all problems pertaining to the patient's welfare. The wards were divided up amongst three of the girls, who would visit their chosen wards twice a week to see that the men were supplied with comfort articles and recreation and to discover if there were any social service problems.

Social service referrals were made to Lucia Irons, the Social Worker, who was responsible for all of the patients. Doctors and nurses would often refer patients who needed counselling or some other social service to the social worker. The men sometimes had problems at home that they felt powerless to do anything about. The Red Cross units at Foxley would be able to contact the Red Cross in the man's hometown and then act as a go-between in the situation. The Red Cross might be asked to make 'home condition' or health and welfare reports, contact relations in England, sort out family problems or the patient's own personal problems or make arrangements when there was a death in the family of a serviceman.

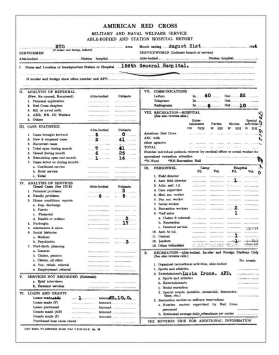

Welfare Report for American Red Cross at Foxley (156th general Hospital Red Cross Archives.)

During August 1944 48 cases were opened by the Red Cross, 41 of which involved the patients and seven involved the staff at the hospital. Three of the cases involved psychiatric histories, and these were referred to the psychiatrist. Three men needed help to write letters home, one had a reading disability, another was dumb and communicated mainly by sign language and the third was blind and also had difficulty in marshalling his thoughts. During the next month 24 new cases were opened, some were personal problems, others were family problems and some were difficulties in adjusting to the way the men's injuries had affected their lives. Helping some of the men was difficult because they were at the hospital for such a short time. Lucia Irons reported:

"We scarcely started working with a man before we find he is to go somewhere else, hence most of our cases have been of the short contact or brief service type." - 156th General Hospital Red Cross Archives.

Lucia Irons was Assistant Field Director as well as Social Worker and in this capacity attended Assistant Field Director meetings twice a month. This meant that she could meet together with Assistant Field Directors of the other four hospitals in the area. These meetings would be quite informal, beginning with supper at the Red Cross Club in Hereford or at a hospital, and afterwards spending the time discussing common problems in an informal manner.

Another responsibility of the Red Cross was to provide emergency loans. Colonel Patton, the Commanding Officer, did not approve of the Red Cross making loans unless the army was unable to pay the men through regular channels. The Colonel ensured that bed patients were paid $10 per month and those on the Rehabilitation Wards, who were able to go into Hereford on a pass, were allocated $30. Any financial needs of the men's families at home were taken care of by the army, as were special payments for birthday or anniversary gifts for families. Lucia Irons reported that the colonel's policy of not allowing the Red Cross to make loans unless the circumstances were exceptional:-

" - caused considerable discontent on the part of some who have spent their pay lavishly or gambled or repaid loans. We feel that the man's self respect and independence is furthered by the policy of each one having his own money and not having to borrow in order to meet expenses." - 156th General Hospital Red Cross Archives.

The Colonel was happy for the Red Cross to lend money in emergency situations. The one loan paid out in July was to a sailor being treated at the hospital. It was thought that he could not be paid by the Army because he was in a different branch of the service. Afterwards it was found that there was a method whereby the Army was permitted to pay men of other branches. Another problem encountered by the Red Cross at Foxley was how to financially assist men of other allied nations like the French patients who were treated at the hospital.

Maude Campbell, one of the recreation workers, was able to speak French fluently and so was able to help the Free French soldiers at the hospital. She was able to interpret for doctors and nurses and teach the patients crafts and games in the wards and in the Recreation Hall. She lent the patients her own French books as well as those in the Red Cross library, which was situated in the Recreation Hall and was regularly taken around the wards.

As well as the Recreation Hall the girls had offices for Red Cross use. Space was a problem to the girls. Lucia Irons reports:

"We have adequate office space and we hope to make our individual offices attractive. Our store space is fairly adequate although a bit crowded; the senior recreation worker has her office there and feels somewhat cramped. The Recreation

Hall, as planned by the architect and executed by the builders, is inadequate. About fifty patients can be seated comfortably for informal recreation; for contests and group games more patients can be accommodated. We are afraid that this building will have to be rationed by the wards." - 156th General Hospital Red Cross Archives.

Red Cross Girls at 52nd General Hospital, using a similar bookcart to that which was used at Foxley (Photo per Mike Webster).

By the end of the year the Red Cross had not been allocated any extra space. Lucia Irons reported that:

"As the program expands we feel more and more cramped" - 156th General Hospital Red Cross Archives.

Colonel Patton went through the official channels to request a larger recreation hall that would be big enough for a games room during the day and a theatre at night, but he had no success. For a short time prior to Christmas the Red Cross had the use of an additional room that could be used as a reception room for patients and visitors, but this was only temporary and after Christmas the situation was as it had been before with patients standing in the hall and visitors waiting in the storeroom.

At the beginning of the 156th's stay at Foxley the Recreation Hall was open daily, morning, afternoon and evening, with the exception of Monday mornings when staff meetings, recreation conferences, individual conferences and general preparations for the week took place. In December the hours were changed so that the Recreation Hall was only open from 1:00 p.m to 8:45 p.m, while the Red Cross Office was open 8:00 a.m. to 5:00 p.m. This decision was made after talking to other units about their usual practice.

Although the Recreation Hall was small a large variety of activities took place there. It had facilities for the men to press and mend their clothes as well as offering entertainment. In August some of the patients helped to enlarge the track and horses of the popular 'Horse Racing Game' to play in the Recreation Hall. The men were able to enlarge all the parts of the game so that the game was six times larger. The Red Cross felt that this activity in itself was combining crafts with recreational improvements. The track was made of green billiard felt and the six-inch horses were made of wood. The men placed their bets with stage money and at the completion of the races those with the most money would win prizes of cigarettes, candy and other comfort articles.

In October an exhibition checkers match was played in the hall. One of the detachment men invited others to try their luck against him while he played ten matches at the same time. In January the visit of a U.S.O. portrait artist caused interest in charcoal and pencil sketching and an exhibition of patient's work was put up in the hall. Lucia Irons describes some of the other activities in her report:

"Bingo, because of the chocolate bar as the prize, seems to be the men's favourite night in the Recreation Room. Other parties have not been so well attended but enjoyed once started. The party of the most fun was one of games such as heels, spit in the ocean, contact and casino." - 156th General Hospital Red Cross Archives.

Saturday night became a 'quiet party' night. Card games were the main entertainment with cocoa and cookies as refreshments. The parties were often run around different themes such as 'Stunt Nite', 'Fun Nite' (silly games), Magician's Evening, Home States Nite, a quiz night and an evening devoted to games of skill. There were musical evenings, one a piano session and another a jam session. The men from the detachment put on a Mills Quartet singing session and the patients produced a night of Hill Billy music.

In October a Halloween Party was attended by 95 patients. The patients decorated the hall with orange and black cut-outs. There were traditional games like apple bobbing and 'bite the apple on the string' and also spoon-feeding and clothes hanging relays. The evening finished up with a blindfold contest. There were prizes for winners in all the events. In addition there was palm reading by one of the nurses. Refreshments consisted of Coca Cola, cake and candy. The programme closed with piano music played by one of the Rehabilitation patients. For Thanksgiving in November there was a Coca Cola party. During the day several Coca Cola parties had taken place on the wards.

Unfortunately the Red Cross were unable to persuade local girls to attend the parties as:

" - the girls available are always taken to dances given at various other units in the area and we are not permitted to have patient dances." - 156th General Hospital Red Cross Archives.

The Red Cross had no separate building for a craft workshop so it was decided to enlist rehabilitation patients to help put up partitions in the work and store-room so that smaller rooms were created. The girls knew that the situation was far from ideal but:

" - it will be better than our present method of 'stealing a corner' of the Recreation Hall." - 156th General Hospital Red Cross Archives.

Even with the limited space the girls managed to offer a wide variety of crafts to the patients. As well as craft materials sent by the American Red Cross R.A.F. Credenhill supplied the unit with scrap metal and other materials to make letter openers, belt buckles and other items. The men also had the opportunity to make coin rings, and bracelets, ward mats and rugs and leather billfolds, cigarette cases, coin purses and picture frames.

'Sweetheart items' of the sort made at 156th General hospital. N.B. Heart is made from plexiglass with coloured insert (Author's Collection).

Some patients made stuffed felt animals for presents for their children. Maude Campbell reports:

"The prize creation of this variety was a very elaborate horse, complete with curly mane and tail and leather saddle and bridle, made by a bed patient." - 156th General Hospital Red Cross Archives.

In October the girls were able to introduce plexiglass to the patients. With this they could make buckles for string belts, picture frames, bracelets, pendants and lapel ornaments. Old toothbrush handles could be used to make the coloured insets for items made from plexiglass.

Recreation was provided on the wards for those who could not leave the ward to attend the Recreation Hall. At first ward recreation took the form of visiting, letter writing and the fulfilling of requests. Bingo games with refreshments were run by Recreation Workers while games of cards, monopoly, dominoes, checkers and Chinese Checkers were organised by the patients themselves.

In November a Public Address system was installed throughout both hospitals on the Foxley site. The 156th and 123rd General Hospitals were two of the fifty hospitals to receive this gift from the American Red Cross. This meant that the patients could listen to public announcements for the station and outside radio stations. There were two wards to each control. Occasionally treatment on one ward might necessitate the cutting off of any noise and so both wards would have to do without the P.A. system.

From October it was possible to show occasional movies on the wards. From January the girls had the use of an additional projector and an operator from the Rehabilitation Section so movies could be shown on a more regular basis.

The girls also took the Special Service Radio and the Red Cross phonograph around the wards to give the patients some music. At one point a concert violinist played the wards to entertain the patients. Two of the Red Cross girls played guitar and were able to play and sing in the wards. In one ward they were accompanied by a blind patient who could play the guitar. The girls felt that this helped to play a part in the man's rehabilitation:

"This particular patient has made a remarkable adjustment to his disability with a strong desire to overcome his handicap. - One day a fellow was washing windows around the patient's bed, and not realizing the patient's condition said, 'How do the windows look?' The patient replied, 'They look all right from here.'" - *156th General Hospital Red Cross Archives.*

The Red Cross was eager to cultivate good relationships with the local community around the hospital. The first contact was with the American Red Cross Club in Hereford. The director there at the time, Mr. Roughgarden, was most helpful in giving advice and directing the girls to resources available to them. The club supported links between the Americans and the British. On 24 June the Hereford times reported on the book drive that the A.R.C. Club had carried out:

"American Red Cross and British Wounded.

The American Red Cross is going to present during this week to the British casualties from Normandy, now at Hereford, over 500 copies of American picture magazines and books, a happy gesture which is bound to give a lot of pleasure to the men at Herefordshire General Hospital. For a fortnight or so the director of the A.R.C. Club in Broad Street (Captain A. Roughgarden of Patterson, New Jersey) and his assistant (Miss Muller of New York City) have conducted a 'Book Drive' among members of the U.S. Forces who readily responded with offers of books and magazines for the British wounded. It is pleasing to recall that something has already been done in the way of making presentations to American wounded when last week the Matron and staff of the Gwynne James Nurses Home in Bridge Street presented flowers for use in brightening up the wards of an American Army Hospital in the West of England." - *Hereford Times 24.06.44. N.B. It is possible that the hospital mentioned was one of the hospitals at Foxley.*

Mr. Roughgarden and the Town Clerk in Hereford, Mr. Gibson, were responsible for forming an Allied Recreation Unit. Four travelling units were

THE HEREFORD TIMES, SATURDAY, JULY

Back From Normandy.—Men wounded in Normandy and now at the Herefordshire General Hospital were presented the other day with magazines, card games, and other pastimes equipment by members of the American Red Cross contingent. Here is the group as photographed at the hospital.

Picture showing Red Cross personnel presenting books to Herefordshire
General Hospital (Hereford Times 24.06.44).

formed to give entertainment in the afternoons and evenings at the British Red Cross hospital and the four American hospitals in the area.

In August an Entertainment Committee for wounded American soldiers was formed in Hereford. Through contact with this committee a tour of the countryside was planned for the patients on a Sunday afternoon. The men were taken to Hay on Wye where the W.V.S. served them tea while they listened to singers and a three-piece orchestra. The women generously insisted that the patients take sandwiches, fruit and cakes, sufficient for two wards back with them. Back at Foxley these were distributed to traction cases that had been unable to make the trip.

The Hereford Entertainment Committee was also able to arrange for groups of English girls to visit on several wards and have refreshments with the ambulatory patients in the Recreation Hall. As Maude Campbell reported:

"The patients help to serve the refreshments and are very enthusiastic about this sort of occasion." - 156th General Hospital Red Cross Archives.

The W.A.A.F. Camp at Credenhill also sent out groups of girls to entertain the patients:

" - which has been greatly appreciated by the men." - 156th General Hospital Red Cross Archives.

Another contact in Hereford enabled the Red Cross to take bathrobe and rehabilitation patients to Vaudeville and Variety shows produced by ENSA.

*The City Arms in Hereford, used as a P.X. and the American
Red Cross Club during the war (M.Collins).*

Because of transportation difficulties Dulcy Goetchius rotated the wards so each could take a turn to attend the shows. Usually 80 patients at a time could attend shows at the Garrison Theatre in Hereford. On one occasion 30 patients were able to attend a matinee performance of the play 'Jane Clegg' in the Red Hill Recreation Centre.

A Mr. Williams of the British Ministry of Information contacted the Red Cross Unit at Foxley and offered to send lectures and entertainment for the patients and also to arrange tours. His offer was gratefully accepted.

The girls also met the Liaison Officer for the British Red Cross in Hereford, Mrs. Norrish. She was able to help with the care of one of the British patients in the hospital and also to work with the American Red Cross in cases involving other British subjects, or in cases where American soldiers were married to British girls. Mrs. Norrish was also able to assist with the problem of supplies at the hospital. She got together a group of women who made 500 bed bags for the hospital from the olive drab towels no longer used by the army. The women also assisted in making curtains for the Recreation Hall.

A Mrs Frances Hinckes was appointed as British Red Cross Liaison Officer for the area local to Foxley to assist in the billeting of British subjects who were related to patients at the hospital. The Red Cross Unit at Foxley was interested in enlisting a group of volunteers from the local area to assist with various Christmas programmes as well as some of the more routine duties that needed doing around the hospital. This would free up some of Lucia Irons's time so that she could spend more time interviewing patients and completing casework. Unfortunately at first Colonel Patton would not sanction a volunteer programme within the hospital, although he was happy for volunteers to work on sewing projects for the patients within their own homes.

In October 1944 there was a meeting between Colonel Patton and Mrs. Hinckes where it was agreed to launch a volunteer programme. Seven volunteers were enlisted. The first training session for the volunteers was held at Mrs. Hinckes's house and took the form of an informal talk on the history and policies of the American Red Cross. The second meeting was held in the workroom of the 156th and the programme consisted of visits to two wards with orientation and explanation by the two ward officers, visits to the patients and a business meeting followed by tea. Colonel Patton and the Chief Nurse were present during refreshments.

The volunteers were given various duties like shopping, sewing and distributing library books. In the period prior to Christmas Colonel Patton sanctioned the enlistment of extra volunteers to help with Christmas activities although he didn't wish the extra volunteers to have contact with the men or wards.

Late in November Christmas preparations commenced. The volunteers made 1,200 Christmas stockings and wrapped 2,000 parcels. The Red Cross planned to place a stocking at the foot of each bed and dress a number of officers and enlisted men as Santa to distribute the presents from around the trees. This plan was dependant on being able to obtain enough Santa costumes.

One of the volunteers, who was a schoolteacher at the village school, planned to bring half of her class for a ward party on Christmas Eve. Two of the other volunteers offered to help. Twenty children attended the party. One or two men were assigned to each child to play 'big brother' for the afternoon. The children played a number of English and American games and ran a contest in which each child had a G.I. partner to take place in a spoon-feeding contest. One of the G.Is entertained the children with magic tricks and Santa Claus gave the children presents of toys, oranges and candy bars. Also on Christmas Eve between 9:00 pm. and 10.00 p.m. a choir of fifty nurses, officers and enlisted men sang carols in each ward.

27 wards took part in a ward and Christmas tree decorating competition, which was judged by Colonel Patton, the chief nurse and the Executive Officer. The craft department had been busy making Christmas tree

ornaments from tin cans, ping-pong balls and painted pinecones. Patients confined to wards made various paper and cellophane ornaments including Santa Claus figures with moving arms and legs, angels made from buckram and paper, paper bells and chains. The four winning wards were awarded a party as a prize. Maude Campbell commented:

"Some of the decorative results were really quite beautiful, as well as ingenious, but the chief value we found in the projects was the numbers of patients involved and the good spirit that was aroused in the wards." - 156th General Hospital Red Cross Archives.

After Christmas the Red Cross was able to enlist six volunteers to work on crafts on the ward and visit the patients. One of the volunteers suggested a new craft idea for the ward patients when she noticed one of the discarded puffball mat frames. She told the Red Cross that her husband had learnt to make scarves on a frame when he was a bed patient in the last war for 4 1/2 months and suggested that he might teach the patients at Foxley. The Red Cross sanctioned the idea so the lady asked her husband who:-

" - consented to divulge the secret which he had jealously guarded from his British friends all these years. He felt quite identified with the soldier whose life in bed was so tedious and sorry for the lads who were so far away from home. Accordingly one night the volunteer and her husband demonstrated the weaving to the thirteen enthusiastic patients." - 156th General Hospital Red Cross Archives.

After meeting the patients her husband decided to become a volunteer himself.

Previous to Christmas there had been some changes of Red Cross Staff. In October Dulcy Goetchius, Senior Recreation worker left the 156th to transfer to Club Service. In her final report Dulcy comments:

"Besides the attempt to set up and operate a program, we, as a staff, have been successful in accomplishing many invaluable contacts with patients and somewhat realize the tremendous need there is for recreation." - 156th General Hospital Red Cross Archives.

Jane Scalborn and Lois Burdette came on temporary detached service to cover the absence but only stayed one week before they were called back to their own unit. Lucia Irons felt that:

"We were very much disappointed that these two workers could not remain with us for the holidays. They were exceptionally well equipped in both background skills and personality. They were like a breath of fresh air to our hospital and were received with great enthusiasm by the Commanding Officer and everyone else in the unit. Our Red Cross staff here felt that they were just what we needed. We have always felt a lack of someone skilled in crafts, particularly and these two girls fitted in very well

with our ideas. We regret that they cannot remain with us, but are hopeful that the future may bring other girls such as they are to us." - 156th General Hospital Red Cross Archives.

On December 13 Mildred Schilling was assigned to the group as Staff Aide. Lucia Irons comments:

"We were very thankful to get some help for our Christmas activities as we wondered how far four of us could encompass the work. Miss Schilling has been a valuable adjunct. She is gay, entertaining, a hard worker, quite unselfish and considerate. The hospital unit personnel and patients have taken a great liking to her. Although we asked for a skilled recreation worker we are quite content as we feel that personality qualifications come first." - 156th General Hospital Red Cross Archives.

Although the Red Cross unit attached to the 156th General Hospital had not had an easy year and had had several obstacles to surmount Lucia Irons was able to report on its work for 1944:

"We feel that our job is a dynamic one, always changing and, we hope, advancing. Our goal has always been satisfaction and contentment on the part of the servicemen and we hope to attain this by keeping them busy in a creative and recreative way and set their minds at rest by helping with family problems." - 156th General Hospital Red Cross Archives.

Chapter 8

123RD GENERAL HOSPITAL
- 'NOTHING LIKE HOME'

Whe 123rd General Hospital arrived at Foxley on the night of July 29 1944. This hospital had been activated at Camp Ellis, Illinois, on 10 March 1944 and on 2 April Lieutenant Colonel Frank McDonald assumed command of the unit.

At this point Lieutenant Colonel McDonald had already had a long career in medicine. He had graduated from the Creighton University School of Dentistry in 1925. In June of this year he was commissioned First Lieutenant in the Officers Reserve Corps. In 1934 he received his M.D. at the University of Colorado and in June 1935 he was transferred to the Medical Corps. From 12 May to 29 December 1943 he served as Commanding

(L.-R.) Lieutenant Ann Sieffart, Lieutenant Colonel Martin Cherasky,
Lieutenant Ruth Link (R.Michtom).

Officer of the 240th Station Hospital, Camp Beale, and from 29 December until 2 April 1944 he served as Commanding Officer of the 128th General Hospital at Camp Cooke, both camps being in California.

While at Camp Ellis, Lieutenant Colonel McDonald interviewed each of the enlisted men of the 123rd. Tom Glennon recalls that he:

" - retained this information and used it to the advantage of the unit and the individual. - To this ability to remember and to understand the problems of his enlisted men is due much to the success of the 123rd General Hospital in its tour of duty overseas in the difficult days of 1944 and early 1945." - The Officers Club - Thomas Glennon.

Lieutenant Colonel Martin Cherasky was appointed Executive Officer of the 123rd. Postwar he was to become head of a New York Hospital and later a Professor of Social Medicine at Einstein Medical School. First Lieutenant Richard O. Penick was appointed Adjutant, his job involved carrying out the orders of the Commanding Officer and overseeing the Personnel Department, which consisted of all the records of the hospital unit.

Tom Glennon reminisces about the personnel of the 123rd who were brought together at Camp Ellis:

"Only war, with its ability to set in motion the necessary forces, could accomplish the tremendous task of gathering together from the corners of our great country the individuals who came to be the very life and breath of our organisation. All of us dropped our associations of a lifetime, separated ourselves from home, office, farm and factory, to contribute our little effort to the formation of an enterprise dedicated to the saving of life and the relief of suffering." - The Officers Club - Thomas Glennon.

Tom Glennon himself was a facio-maxillary surgeon who carried out pioneering facial surgery while in the Dental Section at Foxley. After the war, when he returned to America he became an eminent surgeon and had a hospital named after him.

On 25 June 1944 an advance detachment, composed of three officers: Major Rudley and Lieutenants Wesley and John Dorman with three enlisted men proceeded to the New York Port of Embarkation. On 2 July they set sail and arrived at Liverpool, England, on 15 July. They then travelled to Llandudno, the medical staging camp, where they received the necessary orientation, instructions and theatre administrative and supply directives. This completed, they proceeded to site no. 2 of Camp Foxley to await the arrival of the remainder of the unit.

On 23 July the rest of the unit sailed from New York aboard the Queen Mary, a former luxury liner with the Cunard Line. The Queen Mary had been used for ferrying U.S. troops to the U.K. since August 1942.

An unfortunate incident occurred as the personnel boarded the ship. Seven or eight men from another unit:

" - rebelled at the last moment at the final step from pier to boat. Those who slipped quietly into the river hoping to swim to shore were all apprehended with nothing more serious to alarm them than a good wetting and the prospect of court martial and subsequent incarceration. The one unfortunate soldier who jumped from the gangplank leading to the main deck did not fare so well. The height of the jump and the full equipment, which he carried, caused him to sink immediately. Later, several articles coming to the surface, his hat and his pack among them, it was indicated that he had gone to his death, which end was probably preferable to the terror in his mind at the prospect of battle overseas." - The Officers Club - Thomas Glennon.

The Queen Mary was carrying more than fifteen thousand passengers on this trip but she was to travel without convoy so that she could sail at top speed. Planes gave her an escort out to sea but returned to the mainland when darkness fell. She sailed the usual zigzag course that:

" - made it impossible for submarines to fire at her with any hope of success." - The Officers Club - Thomas Glennon.

The male officers were quartered on the main and A decks and although they had to share rooms and sleep in bunks instead of beds they still considered themselves fortunate in their accommodation. The enlisted men were not so lucky, many slept on the deck or wherever they could find room for their blanket. The troops on board were fed twice a day, at 8 a.m. and 5p.m. and were instructed to take buttered rolls with them when leaving breakfast to eat in between. Tom Glennon recalls:

"I do believe that of all the activities on board - we remember best how wonderful was the food and how plentiful. - The meals were the last exceptional ones we were to have until they were repeated for us a year later on the return voyage on the Queen Elizabeth." - The Officers Club - Thomas Glennon.

Five days later, on the 28 July, the Queen Mary neared Scotland and was escorted into Gouroch by planes. The ship sailed up the Firth of Clyde and gave the men first:

" - a view of the rounded Scottish hills rising on either side, green and beautiful" - The Officers Club - Thomas Glennon.

then the sight of a huge collection of fighting ships of all types in the docks.

A train was waiting to take the men and women on the 12-hour journey to Hereford. The troop train commander of the 123rd was surprised when he saw the British train, likening it to half a dozen stage coach bodies set end to end, quite unlike the American trains that he was accustomed to. The

Panoramic view of 123rd General Hospital (R.Michtom).

Same scene in 1999 (M. Collins).

personnel of the 123rd arrived at Foxley after dark on the night of July 29. Tom Glennon records his feelings on arrival:

"The dark night and the unfamiliar ground, the mud and the confusion of many men in new quarters, combined with complexities at the business of making themselves comfortable and settled in a place that was to be our home through many, many busy months." - The Officers Club - Thomas Glennon.

The next morning, in the light, Tom's impressions of the area changed to:

" - that of open country, farms and woodland, green grass and dense wood, a quiet setting for a work connected with the violence of war." - The Officers Club - Thomas Glennon.

Tom Glennon standing outside one of the huts at Foxley (V. Haines).

Site no. 2 at Foxley had now been completed and consisted of 114 single storey buildings spread over several acres. Most buildings were connected by a series of covered walkways. The roofs of the walkways were supported by regularly placed pillars of cement which were a hazard to the personnel in the early days:

"During complete blackout one moving about without the aid of a torch was in great danger of crashing into those uprights. Many casualties were caused among our personnel, the injuries in particular being crushed noses and discolored eyes." - The Officers Club - Thomas Glennon.

37 of the buildings were used as wards, giving the hospital a maximum capacity of 1442. Robert Masterpolo, a patient with the 123rd, remembers that the wards held about 20 patients on each side. Each ward had at least one private room, a latrine and shower room and a nurse's office at the end of the ward.

The 123rd seemed happier about the conditions at Foxley than the 156th had been. As Colonel Lehman reports in the official archives:

"Physical conditions obtained at this location were excellent, considering that this was a Communications Zone Installation." - 123rd General Hospital Archives. Lieutenant Penick points out that:

"The brick buildings which serve as wards, clinics and administrative headquarters were, in general, in excellent condition and all minor details were remedied. Walls were repainted when necessary and careful attention was given to the pitch mastic floors. Officer's, nurse's and enlisted men's quarters were considered above average. In some respects the stone billets were regarded as superior to the wooden barracks used by this organisation in the United States." - 123rd General Hospital Archives.

Eight buildings had been set-aside for male officer's quarters and nearby was a large building housing the toilet and washing facilities. Tom Glennon describes the view from the officer's quarters:

"Being situated on slightly elevated ground our quarters afforded an excellent view of the immediate countryside. Our hospital area lay in a narrow valley formed between two wooded ridges about two miles apart. This land sloped gently to the mouth of the valley, then, as the ridges ceased, merged with the slightly undulating contour of the surrounding countryside." - The Officers Club - Thomas Glennon.

Tom describes the officer's quarters as:

"Nothing like home but so much better than it might have been" - The Officers Club - Thomas Glennon.

The men soon made the barracks 'home' with beds, footlockers at the side and clothing hanging on improvised racks. Tables were set out for card playing and letter writing. The walls were covered with pin ups and Tom comments about the men who put them up:

"While most of the offenders were medical officers, it is not to be assumed that their inclinations arose from a deep desire to improve their knowledge of anatomy for professional reasons." - The Officers Club - Thomas Glennon.

Some men devised extensions to the electrical systems in the barracks so that bed and table lights could be strung up. Because of the difference between the English and American systems adaptations had to be made so that personal radios could be used.

Each hut had two doors constructed of one-inch board that offered little protection against the cold. Coal stoves warmed the huts albeit not very effectively as the 749th Tank Battalion had discovered the previous winter. Heat was rationed in the huts to four hours per day (4:00 p.m.- 8:00 p.m.). Mary Zeller (nee Casey), a nurse with the 123rd, remembers:

"Once you got your bed warm you didn't come out from under the covers until morning. We had wool army blankets to keep us warm but I can remember sleeping in my uniform many nights just to stay warm enough."

Tom Glennon recalls that:

"What troubled most of us during our stay in England was the inadequacy of the heating system. Those of us old enough to remember the days of the coal stoves in kitchen and parlor of our own homes were startled to learn that we were to go back to that antiquated method of providing warmth" - *The Officers Club - Thomas Glennon.*

He describes the stoves as:

" - cylinder-like contraptions with small openings in top and bottom and no grate, combined with a narrow flue, all too easily obstructed by the products of combustion of soft coal. - We all have

1st Lieutenant Robert Michtom of the 123rd - Winter 1944/45 - (R. Michtom).

memories now of heartbreaking efforts to build satisfactory fires, only to have them splutter for a while, then throw off volumes of heavy smoke which filled quarters and office, followed by the complete collapse of the materials to the bottom of the stove and the necessity of beginning all over again. And when finally the stove was red and its belly filled, our satisfaction was shattered on learning that, without constant care the fire would burn itself out in a couple of hours, leaving a bucket of ashes and a room even colder than before." - *The Officers Club - Thomas Glennon.*

In Tom Glennon's quarters - Building no. 71, Major Travis H. Martin, who was the chief of the Surgical Service took on responsibility for the stove and it was a standard joke that Tom only ever carried in one bucket of coal. Major Martin came from Tennessee and had spent a period of time in Texas so he was particularly susceptible to the cold:

" - particularly the damp, penetrating cold of England. How he used to stand over the pitiful stove, which was ours, striving with all his strength to drive the heavy poker through the mass of fused clinkers, which would constantly plug the narrow opening. The effort was not always confined to the physical side, for often

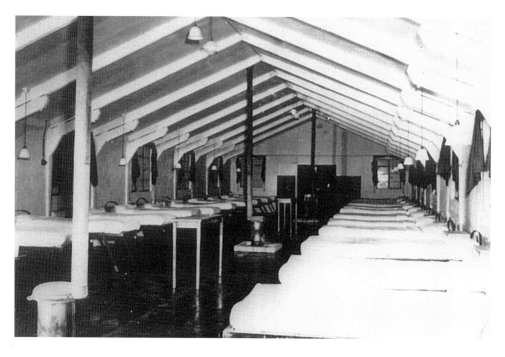

Ward with stove in center (M.Zeller).

the Major attempted a few choice words to hurry along the process." - *The Officers Club - Thomas Glennon.*

Major Martin would often successfully demonstrate his fire lighting technique for the other personnel of the 123rd. The one notable exception was the time a visiting colonel came to watch the demonstration.

"It was unfortunate that the stove pipe had become plugged at that particular moment, causing the room to fill completely with smoke, which result caused us all to vacate for a period of fifteen minutes. After that the major battered the stove pipe violently enough to discharge two buckets of soot." - *The Officers Club - Thomas Glennon.*

The nurses were housed in 12 similar barracks. Mary Zeller recalls them as being 'cramped'. Each hut had eight to ten beds. Clothes and personal items were kept in a footlocker at the foot of the bed. Mary was unhappy about the fact that there were no bathroom facilities in the huts. She remembers:

"We had to go outside and up a hill to the bathroom. We were able to have good hot water for our bathtub. However, once you took your hot bath you made a B. line from the bathroom to the hut and jumped into bed. I remember if we had to 'tinkle'

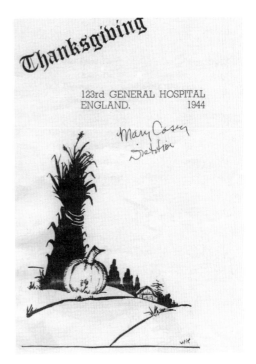

Left - Sergeant Williams, Head Chef with Mary Casey. (M.Zeller).
Right - Menu for Thanksgiving Celebrations 1944 (M.Zeller).

in the night we would go outside in the dark and squat and take a leak rather than run up the hill to the bathroom facilities. Some of the women got caught doing that and there was soon a sign put up that we were not allowed to do that anymore."

The site had three mess halls, one for enlisted men, one for officers and nurses and the third for patients. Each mess hall had one mess officer, three hospital dieticians, one mess steward and one mess sergeant. Although usually the officers and enlisted men ate separately one member of the personnel, Private Sooner, ate alongside the officers. Private Sooner was a black kitten adopted by the nurses of the 123rd. Beverley Wilbert remembers that when she heard the food cart coming she would rush in for her meal.

All mess halls displayed posters with appeals to conserve food. The Officer of the Day had the task of checking the wastage during each meal. This had the effect of diminishing food waste by at least half. The hospital provided the transport for the rations, which came from the nearby General Depot at Moreton on Lugg. Fresh vegetables were also delivered to supplement the regular menu. Tom Glennon remembers that the:

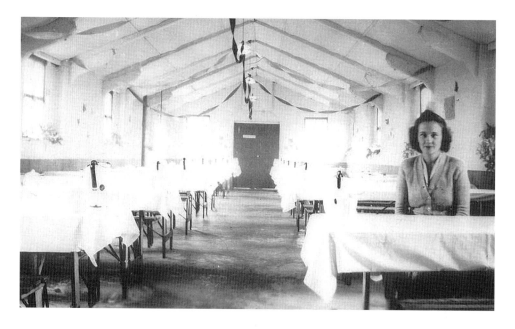

Mess Hall decorated for Thanksgiving with paper turkey decorations (M. Zeller).

" - *Officer's Mess Hall in its original state was not inviting. A rough interior, unfinished walls and bare wooden tables and chairs provided a poor background for the enjoyment of our food. Inadequate serving tables in the early days and the inconvenient facilities for washing our mess gear in the kitchens apparently gave justification for the grumbling of some officers. But even for this there was some excuse - poor planning of construction, lack of sufficient help in the kitchen and almost complete absence of the necessary serving containers. - Bringing about the improvement was long and difficult but gradually the crude surroundings and the objectionable features of serving were replaced.*

The wall dividing the Mess Hall was removed, curtains were placed at the windows, table cloths, chinaware and cutlery provided and a large serving table with appropriate dishes set up in the center of the kitchen end of the large room. The wash line was eliminated and our handling of dishes confined to carrying them to the small opening in the kitchen wall where they were taken care of by the Mess Personnel.

The original cups and plates were metal with an enamel covering. Under the pressure of heavy use and constant washing, the enamel chipped easily and found its way into our food and our coffee. A suggestion from Captain Kalmanowitz, that the Officers Club fund could be used to purchase chinaware, was received favourably by

Colonel McDonald and the board of Governors. T. W. Rutter of Widemarsh Street, Hereford, supplied chinaware of a kind and number sufficient to take care of two hundred people. The original expenditure was about seventy pounds, but the heavy breakage necessitated constant replenishing and of course heavy expenditure. But it was agreed, after a few days use of the new service, that the most important step in improving the Mess Hall had been taken." - The Officers Club - Thomas Glennon.

For special occasions, such as Thanksgiving, the Mess Halls were decorated appropriately and special menus were produced. Mary Zeller remembers that for Thanksgiving 1944 the lunchroom was decorated:

" - with crepe paper on the ceiling, white tablecloths on the tables and each table had something setting on it for decoration. - We decorated with whatever we could to make things more appealing for the troops."

Chapter 9

123RD GENERAL HOSPITAL
- SUPERIOR RATINGS

The 123rd General Hospital was officially opened for patients on 4 August 1944. The first train-load of patients was transferred from a hospital train at Moorhampton Station to the camp by ambulance and bus. The first time this procedure was carried out it took two hours but with each new convoy there was an increase in the efficiency and speed of this phase of the process. Up to March 1945 the hospital received three to five convoys per week.

SURGICAL SERVICE

Each section of the hospital was allotted a number of buildings. 23 wards were assigned for the use of the Surgical Service and three intermediate wards were kept available for the service requiring the greater number of beds at the time. The Surgical Service supervised an anesthetic and operating room, physiotherapy department, central supply and sections for general surgery, septic surgery, orthopedics, genito-urinary and E.E.N.T. clinic. Steam heat was piped to the surgery and E.E.N.T. clinic from the boiler room located in the hospital area.

From 7 August to 31 December 1944 2,955 patients were admitted to the Surgical Service of the 123rd and 975 operations were performed, the first being a secondary closure by the Chief of Surgical Service and a ward officer.

On 10 October 1944 the hospital was designated genito-urinary center for 5th Hospital Group with Major Martin serving as regional consultant. 36 operations were performed in this section in 1944, only one was considered to be major. 45 cystoscopes and 13 pylograms were carried out.

PHYSIOTHERAPY SECTION

The Physiotherapy section of the 123rd was staffed by two physiotherapists and three enlisted men. Its remit was to treat diseased and rehabilitate injured parts. When the hospital opened this section had no electricity or hot water, but this was rectified one week later so that the section could make use of the machinery which gave out ultra-violet rays and luminous and non-luminous infra-red rays. It also used whirlpool baths, sinus-oidal, galvanic and faradic currents in its treatment of patients.

To meet the requirements of the patients this section needed to be innovative in making equipment:

"One improvisation was a bicycle mounted on a wooden frame. By substituting a steel shaft for the front wheel the bicycle was made stationary and the height of the base of the frame was great enough to give the rear wheel movement. By increasing or decreasing the pedal tension the physiotherapists were enabled to give patients leg exercises, which ordinarily would have been omitted.

Rubber strips cut from discarded bicycle tubes were nailed to wooden blocks in such a manner as to present openings for the insertion of fingers. This item of equipment proved satisfactory in exercising the muscles and tendons of the hand." - 123rd General Hospital Archives.

REHABILITATION SECTION

The Rehabilitation Section put their section into operation immediately after the first hospital train was received. A daily training schedule was devised and followed, permitting convalescent patients to test their physical condition and endurance with the view to returning physically and mentally fit troops to combat. A calisthenics programme was executed daily and patients were given other means to restore strength to their bodies, such as punch bags. Services of recuperating soldiers were utilised in the construction of a miniature golf course near the Rehabilitation Wards. Hikes were also taken under the supervision of an assigned officer.

LABORATORY SERVICE

The Clinical Laboratory Service opened on 2 August 1944. A volunteer blood donor service, which 275 enlisted men volunteered for, was established by the Laboratory Service. In January 1945 a collecting team from the E.T.O. Blood Bank spent two days at the hospital soliciting voluntary contributions from type O donors on behalf of the men wounded on the front lines. Response to this appeal exceeded the quota established by the blood bank.

At the beginning wide cracks in the walls of the laboratory building and the presence of a ventilator made the bacteriology room draughty but this deficiency was soon corrected. The personnel built shelves, stands and cabinets and converted many of the fixtures to more practical uses. There were some problems with the laboratory equipment. It was necessary to replace the plugs of all American made electrical equipment with British plugs, even though a 110-volt transformer had been installed. The heating unit of the standard gasoline model incubator was also unsatisfactory as it required air pressure to be replaced every two hours and needed refueling every four hours. It was replaced with a kerosene burner similar to the one used in the kerosene refrigerator, which was provided.

The Laboratory Service encountered a more serious problem at the beginning of 1945 when a fire destroyed the interior of the laboratory building. An investigation found that the fire was caused by the heat of a stove igniting a wooden part of the building. The fire spread to the roof and walls before being discovered and the rear of the building was badly gutted before the fire was brought under control. The fire was extinguished by laboratory personnel and men on night duty. A rebuilding programme was quickly initiated and the laboratory was formally opened on 4 March. During the rebuilding process the Laboratory Service continued functioning.

X-RAY SECTION

The X-ray building at Foxley was composed of two large technique rooms, a dark room and two offices. The department had a number of pieces of equipment: a keleket machine, a stereo cassette charger, a field localisation unit, two mobile solus units, a Picket field unit and a portable Watson Unit, Westinghouse field processing unit, auxiliary wash tanks, electric drying cabinet, loading bins, cassettes and hangers. It was necessary for the enlisted men of the department to construct desks and files from boxes and generally clean up the buildings before the department could function properly.

As the first convoy of patients arrived films were collected from the train and, after identifications were checked the films were entered in files. From 12 September 1944 films were made a part of the patient's records and were kept on the wards. From October all films remained with the patients during transportation from the train to respective wards. A detail from the department collected the films by wards and marked each set up with the ward numbers. They were then processed and notes made to suggest any special procedure that might be advisable and to guide the ward officers in the necessity of re-examination. It was found that the average 300 patient convoy could be checked in this manner and that films could be made available on the wards in 12 hours or less.

DENTAL SECTION

The Dental Clinic was opened immediately after the unit arrived at Camp Foxley. Bracket tables, desks and laboratory tables were constructed by the enlisted men assigned to the department. Heat was a problem in the clinic:

"The stoves being very small and without attention from five in the afternoon until seven in the morning it was impossible to hold the fire overnight so each day the routine was repeated - search for wood and paper, a flame and failure, finally success and the brave little stove would strive to cast a breath of warm into the chilly atmosphere of the clinic. How cold it could be in that particular building can be understood when it is mentioned that on a couple of occasions the water in the developing tank showed a crust of ice. In the surgery room of the clinic a hot plate

Left - Tony Di'Resta of the 123rd 1945 (M.Zeller).
Right - Eddie Vzedenburgh of the 123rd 1945 (V.Haines).

was set on end by the windowsill and insignificant as it was it did offer the operator a chance to relieve the numbness in his fingers during the early hours of the morning." - Officer's Club - Thomas Glennon.

During October a large influx of patients overburdened the small dental staff of five officers but high standards were maintained. The workload was further increased when the dental clinic was required to treat members of units without dental clinics in the area. The prosthetic section of the Dental Clinic encountered extra difficulties when patients returning from the battlefronts had become separated from their barracks bags in which they had put their appliances.

More problems were encountered by the Dental Clinic in rainy weather. Because of the inadequacy of the sewage and drainage system the sewers became stopped up and sewage backed into the dental clinic and laboratory. During October 1944 the problem was so acute that operations in the dental clinic were suspended temporarily. The clinic was flooded three times during November. During rainy weather the entrance of the Headquarters Building was flooded by waves running down from the paved driveway near the building. It was necessary to dig drainage ditches and place additional drainage pipes to remedy the problem.

NURSES

The mission of the nurses at this hospital was to provide a high level of patient care. To this end the Principal Chief Nurse appointed three nurses as supervisors. Lilian Ostrand was the Assistant Chief Nurse, her duties consisted of sorting out problems met by the nursing staff and dealing with any other circumstances that interfered with the provision of high quality nursing care.

Day supervisors coordinated the nursing service and gave advice and assistance as necessary. At night nurses reported to the night supervisor for instruction and informed her of emergencies. Each morning before being relieved the night supervisor made written

Lieutenant Mary Casey (Hospital Dietician) with two of the chefs (M. Zeller).

reports on the condition of all seriously ill or unusual cases. Ward Supervisors took responsibility for each ward.

Mary Zeller (nee Casey) was a Hospital Dietician, her duties included ordering food and kitchen supplies. Because of the food-rationing situation in England most of the supplies were shipped from the States. She recalls that:

"Many times the hams and meats were very salty. It was during the rationing time in the United States. Most of our food was canned or dried. Around the holidays we would get more fresh vegetables and fruit."

As a dietician Mary also supervised and prepared meals, planned special diets for the injured and visited the patients.

Corporal Coward, cook with Mary Casey 1945 (M.Zeller).

SUPPLY SECTION

At the opening of the hospital Central Supply Section had only one building. Two ward tents and four pyramidals were erected to supplement the original storage space for medical supplies. This department had an autoclave that supplied the clinics and wards with sterile dressings, instruments and solutions. The enlisted personnel of this section spent their free time putting up shelves, cupboards and indirect lighting in the operating room. They also painted the surgery, constructed sidewalks and planted grass around the outside of the buildings. Groups were detailed daily to improve the appearance of the grounds. Areas were levelled or built up accordingly.

Soon after the 123rd arrived in the U.K. the Quartermaster Supply Department found that not all accommodation stores were issued, some were to be procured from British sources. British officials were interviewed and a small amount of supplies were obtained. It was necessary to find the small amount of office furniture needed from American sources.

The 123rd was assigned to General Depot G22 (Moreton on Lugg, Herefordshire) for Class 1 and 2 supplies. However, as that depot was contemplating closure there was a shortage of many Class 2 supplies. It was necessary to source these from elsewhere, causing additional burdens on transportation. In November 1944 the unit was assigned to General Depot G24 (Honeybourne, Worcestershire) but many items of clothing and equipment were not available there either. Because of this the unit was assigned to G35 (Bristol, Somerset). Even with these arrangements there was still a shortage of many items.

Every effort was made to conserve supplies at the hospital. Directives were published on conservation of coal and coke and on precautions to take to prevent water wastage:

"In December 1944 a campaign to conserve rubber tires was promoted in accordance with instructions from higher headquarters. Spot announcements were made over the public address system and pertinent paragraphs were inserted in the Daily Bulletin, official publication of the hospital. A contest was held and the prizes were awarded to personnel writing the best essays on the subject, and to the artist submitting the best poster." - 123rd General Hospital Archives.

TRAINING

While the 123rd was at Foxley it was necessary for all of the personnel to attend training sessions. A 'Plans and Training Officer' was appointed to formulate a training program for officers and nurses. Training films and film strips were used extensively in training and in some cases battle experienced infantry officers and enlisted men lectured to patients and members of the Medical Department.

Chemical Warfare defence measures were taken shortly after the arrival of the unit in the U.K. Part of the training schedule required wearing a gas mask for half an hour each week and classes were held in which demonstrations of defence against chemical attack were given by an officer and non-commissioned officer who had attended special courses. A gas alarm system was established throughout the area and all personnel were instructed in the method of its operation

From time to time officers and enlisted men were detailed to attend various schools, which included courses in dentistry, chemical warfare, bomb reconnaissance, treatment of gas casualties and anesthesia. The Laboratory Service of the 123rd hosted a Clinical Conference that took place on 28 October 1944.

Training of a different type took place at Foxley in 1945 as six cases of Venereal Disease were discovered.

"Monthly physical inspections were conducted and talks made to all personnel at periodic intervals by the chaplain, the Executive Officer and the Commanding

Officer. Training films on this subject were frequently shown and the army booklet 'You Don't' Know' was issued to all personnel on 29 June following the showing of a V.D. film." - 123rd General Hospital Archives.

INSPECTIONS

In 1945 there were frequent inspections of the hospital plant and area. The enlisted men's barracks were inspected daily and officers quarters were inspected each Saturday morning by the Hospital Commander. As a result of one inspection a campaign to maintain the cleanliness of the mess gear was instituted:

"Meat cans, covers, cups, knives, forks and spoons were displayed daily on the beds of all enlisted men and inspected each morning and afternoon. Disciplinary action was taken against those men whose mess gear was considered below the prescribed standard of cleanliness." - 123rd General Hospital Archives.

Regular inspections were carried out at the two hospitals at Foxley during 1944-45. The 156th received the inspections with reluctance as the Commanding Officer stated:

"Some emphasis should have been given to hospital inspections - the whys and wherefores - this would have encouraged earlier, more gracious acceptance of inspections in general." - 156th General Hospital Archives.

The 123rd fared better and in November and December 1944 it was awarded two 'superior' ratings. On 3 January 1945 there was a meeting of Hospital Commands and Chief Nurses of 5th Hospital Group at Foxley:

"Anticipating a tour of the hospital plant by all visiting officers, hospital personnel worked with increased effort and interest to complete the program of improving the physical appearance of the buildings and the area. Signs were erected throughout the hospital to guide the inspecting party through the various departments, and all painting projects were completed. However rainy weather abbreviated the inspection with only a few of the buildings being visited, bringing great disappointment to the officers and men of the organisation. All visiting officers nevertheless proffered their thanks to the Commanding Officer of the 123rd General Hospital in appreciation of the preparation made by the unit." - 123rd General Hospital Archives

AWARDS

Several of the personnel of the 123rd received medals while at Foxley. In 1944 47 enlisted men of the 123rd received Good Conduct medals for 'exemplary behaviour, efficiency and fidelity.' On 29 May 1945 Technical

Sergeant William W. Hepler of the Medical Detachment was awarded a Certificate of Merit in recognition of meritorious service as N.C.O. in charge of surgery at the 123rd.

Major Harrison E.Law, Chief of the Orthopedic Section was awarded a Certificate of Merit for:

"The professional skill displayed by Captain Law as senior surgeon aboard L.S.T. No. 335 from 30 May 1944 to 23 June in administering to casualties, generally mitigating the suffering and contributing immeasurably to minimizing the loss of life among our wounded fighting during the early days of the invasion of France." - 123rd General Hospital Archives

Private Leonard Paladino of the Medical Detachment was awarded a Bronze Star for:

" - distinguishing himself by heroic achievement in action against the enemy while serving with the Ninth Infantry Division on 10 October 1944 during the operation in Germany." - 123rd General Hospital Archives

Two other enlisted men were given awards for the work they carried while on the battlefield.

Chapter 10
A MILLION DOLLAR WOUND

Thousands of patients passed through the three hospitals based at Foxley and many soldiers owed their life to the care they received at first the 99th, then the 156th and 123rd General Hospitals. 1st Lieutenant Richard Penick, Adjutant of the 123rd recalls:

" - the emotional feeling experienced when the hospital trains pulled into the little station near our hospital and our personnel began unloading the casualties that were sent to our hospital for treatment. It was gratifying to see these patients after treatment go back to duty or to the States for further treatment or rehabilitation. It is my understanding that not one patient died while under our care. Most remarkable!"

Captain Thomas A. Harkins, of the Medical Section, gave a high standard of care to his officer patients. Tom Glennon recalls:

Captain Thomas A. Harkins of the Medical Section (R.Michtom).

"The chubby Captain not only offered a fine branch of medical treatment, but also provided a kitchen and dining service second to none. It is a well-known fact that one of the requirements of the wardmen on Wards 27 and 28 was an ability to make apple pie. From somewhere the Captain procured apples and the other necessary ingredients, and the stage was set for another fattening feast. Captain Harkins was a native of Texas and in his heart there burned a fierce devotion to his home state. Few of our number knew that in his luggage he carried a full size flag

of Texas, and that on occasion he stated that if he ever died overseas it was his wish to be buried in its voluminous folds. - In fact when he did die Thomas Harkins was buried wrapped in his flag.

In the early days of our Officer's Club when officer patients were required to have sponsors, Captain Harkins would issue a group invitation to those under his care and lead them on to the fun and liquid refreshment. On those few occasions when the genial Captain lingered a bit too long at the bar, he was taken in tow by Major Rubright. The latter lost his charge on the way to quarters one Saturday night, for whereas the Major believed that cement walks were made for use, Captain Harkins thought a straight line was the shortest distance between the club door and his bunkhouse. All this occurring during the rainy season, the area between walks was a sea of red sticky mud, which soon caused the wanderer to stop and flounder and fall. One can imagine the damage done to green blouse and pinks - Light beige coloured trousers as a result." - The Officer's Club - Thomas Glennon.

One of Harkin's patients in Ward 27 was Jim Polk. Tom Glennon remembers:

"He was more sick than ever he realised at the time. The first few days following his operation he was the color of manila paper, but both color and appetite improved after he was induced to try a glass of what appeared to be sweet cider, but what was really champagne. For a time coordination was lost as well as Jim's ability to articulate with any semblance of clarity but the lapse was only temporary. From that moment Jim was on the upgrade and in a short time was back on duty again. Proper postoperative treatment can do wonders." - The Officer's Club - Thomas Glennon.

Another patient, Robert Kauffman, of the 3rd Armored Division, recalls his stay at Hospital Plant 4178:

"The newly finished hospital had been empty, waiting for the first flood of casualties that would pour across the English Channel after our forces had landed somewhere on the Continent of Europe.

But now D-Day had come and gone, and the Allied Armies had landed on the beaches of Normandy. In the weeks that followed, Army ambulances would make their endless circuits between the docks of south England and the hospital to unload their mutilated cargo. As soon as the airstrip was completed on the top of Omaha Beach, airfields in south England were added to the collection points for the casualties that were flown to England and brought to the hospital by ambulance. It was by the route of Omaha Beach Airstrip that I found myself in this hospital. I had suffered a gunshot wound of the abdomen and some shrapnel wounds from a Panzerfaust on July 10 in Normandy.

The weeks that I spent in hospital were a tranquil interlude after the tumultuous preceding weeks of rapid movement and intense action. The large, freshly painted ward was already filled to capacity and was always alive with the banter of unquenchable G.I. humor and ongoing teasing with the nurses. If there seemed to be an air of exaggerated laughter, even among the more seriously wounded, it was simply the outpouring of sheer joy, the exhilaration of just being alive. After all, these men were the survivors of that still perilously clung-to Normandy Beach-head.

There were men from the 1st, 4th and the 29th Divisions, who had made the assault on Omaha and the Utah Beaches. There was a Ranger or two who had participated in taking the German position on the precipitous Point Du Hoc. There were glider men and paratroops from the vaunted 82nd and 101st Airborne Divisions who had fought in isolation, exploiting enemy weaknesses to gain their vital objectives. There were men from other units such as the 3rd Armored Division who joined the battle later, and who had their baptisms of fire in the fierce battle of the hedgerows where every field was transformed into an enemy fortress and the murderous crossfire took an unconscionable toll of lives.

In the bed beside me was a young soldier who still trembled with fear. After being seriously wounded he had lain in his foxhole beneath the dead body of a fellow soldier for two days. In another bed close by was a glider man with an extremely heavy accent from the 82nd Airborne. He told us how he had paraded before Mussolini as a young soldier in the Italian Army until his mother was able to smuggle him out of Italy to the U.S. He told us about his glorious entry into France, how, when his glider hit the ground, it broke up on impact and he was hurled through the air, only to come to a sliding halt with his face half buried in the manure of a Norman cow. There was another man across the aisle from me who filled only half his bed. He had been run over by a tank and had his legs amputated below the hips. He stared stoically at the ceiling for hours on end to avoid the painful downward glance at the flat taut blanket where his legs and feet should have been.

A special bond quickly developed among the men in the ward. Strong friendships were quickly forged. The ambulatory patients would move among those who were bedfast, encouraging them, asking them about their units, hoping to find mutual acquaintances within their ranks. They would light cigarettes for those who were helpless and run small, necessary errands.

There were men in all manner of casts, some in body casts, others in leg casts that were elevated in traction and still others in arm casts, with the arms locked forward of the body in crooked positions, appearing like mimes frozen in mid-performance.

There was always a significant change of mood among the men in the ward as night approached. It was a puzzling phenomenon. Was it the fear of the isolation that quiet and darkness bring? Was it the apprehension of each man receding into his own private arena of hell, where in sleep, the subconscious mind would resurrect a thousand different scenarios of torment that he had already endured?

During the night there were frequent periods of unusual quiet when I would suppress sleep and in an almost childlike manner, surrender myself to the marvelous security of the ward. I would try to fasten my mind on enjoying the soft, clean comfort of the hospital bed. I would listen to the gentle rhythm of my own breathing, the most elementary and gratifying reminder of being alive. For me, to be awake was the dream, to sleep was the nightmare.

Often my reverie was intruded upon by the audible torment of those who slept. There would be a sudden outburst as someone in a nightmare gave out a pathetic cry for help. Another would curse loudly in a frenzy of helplessness over a weapon that would not fire; someone else screamed orders to a squad that did not exist. To hear, welling out of the darkness, the pleading plaintive cry of a man calling for a friend who would not answer, was almost heartbreaking.

Meanwhile, up and down the long darkened ward, deep into the night, there would be sporadic clicks and flashes of cigarettes held between the quivering lips of men who had become hostages to that felt clutch of sleeplessness. For the sleepless, as well as the sleeping fell victim to the torments of the night. Unrepentant darkness, which knows neither truce nor armistice would relentlessly do its demon work, constantly awaking the fear-laden memories of battlefield terror. Unforgetting, unforgiving darkness, with a sly viciousness, would again and again lacerate those tender, unsutured inner wounds and would not let them heal. And those nights would be the cruel harbinger of decades of similar nights to come, when time and distance would neither diminish nor assuage the unremitting pain.

During the night there was always the sound of nurses on constant patrol, quietly and efficiently moving among the beds with their flashlights, checking on each man. At some beds there were extended pauses as they whispered consolingly to those who could not sleep. To others, with the same comforting tenderness, they administered medication when the pain was no longer bearable.

The flick of the light switch in the morning, accompanied by the cheery voices of the day nurses, signaled the distinct change of the mood that would restore the easy lightheartedness that made the days so different and almost pleasant.

One day the daily routine of the ward was interrupted with a great stir of excitement. A full Colonel and his party had come to the hospital. When the Colonel and his entourage entered our ward, we found out that he had come to present the Purple Heart to each of us. What made this particularly auspicious was that this was the first time the awards had been made in a hospital since the Normandy invasion.

Those of us who were ambulatory were ordered to stand in front of our beds, while the Colonel's Aide read the names and the serial numbers and then the

Colonel made the presentation. What a motley and unmilitary looking group we must have been, standing in front of our beds, dressed in our pajamas, bathrobes and canvas hospital slippers.

When the Colonel followed by his splendidly attired entourage, took his position in front of me, he paused and looked at me. He then asked, "How old are you son?" "Eighteen years old, Sir." I replied. "What the hell are you doing over here?" he bellowed out across the ward. I replied, "I'm just very proud to be here."

Some weeks later I underwent another operation. In Normandy, in the field hospital, when the projectile had been removed from my abdomen the wound was stuffed with Vaseline gauze to ensure proper healing. Now that the wound had healed properly, a second operation was needed to close the wound.

Following the operation I was placed alone in a room. One day the door suddenly opened and several nurses burst into my room singing 'Happy Birthday.' One of the nurses had seen on my records that August 7 was my nineteenth birthday, so they had brought me small gifts. Such thoughtfulness and personal concern in the midst of their uniquely busy and demanding schedule was a most moving experience. It showed what a special breed of people they really were." - The Normandy ward - R. F. Kauffman.

Soon after this Robert was able to rejoin D Co. of the 36th Armored Regiment of the 3rd Armored Division, on the Continent.

Another patient at Foxley was Robert Masterpolo. He was with the 10th Infantry Regiment, 5th Infantry Division, which was part of General Patton's 3rd Army. He recalls his journey from France to Foxley:

"I was wounded on 20 September 1944 near Metz, France. I went back to our Battalion Aid Station first, then by ambulance to a Field Hospital in tents. I will always remember seeing a dead lieutenant on a stretcher outside the entrance to the tent. The medics were very busy at the time as there was a tough battle going on near Metz. My wound in my upper right arm was rebandaged and I was probably given a shot of penicillin. From there we rode by ambulance to Verdun where they had set up a French hospital.

After a week there I got my first airplane ride (in a C.47 Dakota) to England and wound up at the 123rd. I had what us infantry men called 'A Million Dollar Wound,' which is just serious enough to get us out of the front line and back to the hospital where we had clean beds, hot food and good looking nurses that could speak English."

Bob recalls one memorable hot meal at Foxley that consisted of Chilli Con Carne with lots of beans in it. He tells the story:

"All of us were quite familiar with some artillery terms. The men would give a target, range etc. and request a fire mission. One of the patients would say 'On

(L-R) Unknown patient, Robert E. Masterpolo, I. A. Kobza (R. Masters).

the Way' and let a burst of flatulence go. The lights were out on the ward and the duty nurse was in her office. One highly talented patient called out, 'Fire the battery for effect,' and let out a string of explosions that had the ward roaring with laughter. The nurse came out and said, 'What's going on out here?' No one volunteered an answer."

Bob remembers several of his fellow patients. Many of them had shrapnel wounds and some had casts on arms and legs. He recalls that one man in the ward had been shot in his left chest by a German officer with a pistol. He was lucky as the bullet went straight through his body and came out under his arm without hitting a vital organ. Another man, who was a combat engineer with the 9th Infantry division, had a blasting cap explode while he was holding it, so his hand had brass fragments embedded in it. The doctors were trying to remove the fragments so that he could flex his fingers and use his hand again.

One infantry soldier Bob got friendly with was named Kobza and came from Milwaukee. Kobza was from the 29th Infantry Division and was in hospital for the second time. The first time he had been wounded was on Omaha Beach on D.Day. Kobza sent a photo of himself and Bob back home with Bob's name and address on it. Sadly, when Bob was back with his unit, he received a letter from Kobza's brother informing him that Kobza had been killed in action on the Continent when he rejoined his unit for the third time.

Left - Gwen Deeley, the girl Robert Masterpolo met in Birmingham (R.Masters).
Right - W.A.A.F., Joy Memmot, based at R.A.F. Credenhill (R.Masters).

Another patient Bob became friendly with was a man named Zett, nicknamed Tex as he came from Texas. He was from a Tank Destroyer Battalion and had a shrapnel wound in his shoulder. The nurses used to mistake the two friends for brothers as they were both tall and dark haired with moustaches. Zett had also pulled a tendon loose in his leg. While it was healing the doctors put a cast on his leg and kept him in bed.

One day, as Bob had a pass to go to Hereford he stopped to see Tex on his way out of the ward. Tex asked Bob to get the doctor, as he wanted to relieve himself. Bob recalls:

"I asked the nurse on duty if Tex could see a doctor. She wanted to know why so I said, 'Tex doesn't want me to tell you.' She replied, 'Well, you had better tell me.' A Pfc. didn't argue with a lieutenant so now my problem was how to tell a lady without using bad words like 'pee'. I finally said, 'Tex can't pass his water.' She said she would take care of it. I thought, 'I sure have lost a buddy on this deal.' On my way back from town I stopped to see Tex and apologize for telling the nurse his secret. He wasn't mad and sure felt better."

Robert Masterpolo and A.T.S. girlfriend, Marianne Banks.

There was also a young French boy in Bob's ward. He couldn't speak English so Bob couldn't ask him how he came to be at Foxley. Each night the nurses would tuck the boy up. This would lead to the other patients asking if they could be tucked in too.

Unfortunately, while at Foxley Bob's wound got infected so it was necessary to drain it regularly and change the dressings each day. Because the medical staff couldn't remove the piece of shrapnel the wound took longer to heal. Until it healed Bob couldn't leave the hospital for longer than a day. One of the nurses, 2nd Lieutenant Azalee Simmons, suggested that Bob ask a doctor for a three-day pass so that he could spend it with her and another nurse. The two nurses could change the dressings on his wound for him while he was away from the hospital. Unfortunately Bob did not dare to ask the doctor for a pass as enlisted men were not allowed to date officers.

While at Foxley Bob did have one 48-hour pass, which he spent in Birmingham. He remembers staying at a large Red Cross Centre there. While there he met and dated a girl named Gwen Deeley from Cradley Heath. While on a pass in Hereford Bob remembers having a date with a W.A.A.F. named Joy Memmot from nearby Credenhill. He met her when she visited Bob's ward. She gave Bob her cap badge as a souvenir. Bob also dated an

A.T.S. girl, Marianne Banks, who was stationed in a large house in Hereford.

She gave Bob her photo with an inscription on it, but Bob found that she didn't mean what she wrote on the photo as:

"When I went to call on her she was out with another fellow. We had lots of competition in those days."

Bob spent Thanksgiving dinner in England, then left from Southampton for LeHavre where he caught up with his old outfit in the Ruhr area of Germany just in time to participate in the movement of the 3rd Army to Luxembourg. He recalls that:

"We had a lot of casualties crossing the Moselle River and gave the 123rd General Hospital a lot of business."

Bob received his Purple Heart medal while at Foxley. After leaving the 123rd and rejoining his unit on the Continent he carried the paperwork for the award around with him folded into his wallet, hence the creases.

While at the 123rd and 156th General Hospitals most patients received Purple Heart Medals for being wounded in action. On 17 March 1945 the 123rd General Hospital actually ran out of Purple Heart medals, which is an indication of the large number of patients treated at the hospital. The Commanding Officers of the two hospitals also awarded Silver Star Medals to those who had distinguished themselves in the face of the enemy.

Robert Masterpolo 2004 (R.Masters).

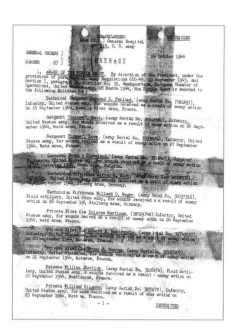

Awards notice for Purple Heart Medals at Foxley 14.10.1944 (R.Masters).

Chapter 11

123RD GENERAL HOSPITAL
- AMERICAN RED CROSS

On August 9 1944 the American Red Cross Staff for the 123rd General Hospital arrived at Foxley. The staff consisted of: Isabel Knaus, Assistant Field Director; Lois Joseph, secretary; Evelyn Shieber, Senior Recreation Worker and Frances Thomas, Staff Aide. Like the Red Cross unit attached to the 156th the girls were housed in the nurse's quarters and had the use of two other buildings, one contained offices, a storage room and a craft room and the other was a Recreation Hall. The Recreation Hall was opened up as soon as possible to the patients who were:

" - eager for anything that might break the monotony of hospital life." - 123rd General Hospital Red Cross Archives.

At the beginning the hall had just four easy chairs, two bookcases, a number of benches and a ping-pong table. Frances Thomas took on the job of decorating the room with brightly coloured tablecloths and maps and pictures donated from staff member's footlockers. Curtains were made for the windows and one of the patients, an Indian boy who held a D.S.C., drew a series of Sad Sack pictures on the walls using watercolours. One of the men from the 123rd made large divisional plaques to display around the room and a patient made divisional book was placed in the Recreation Hall, its purpose being to bring together men from the same outfit.

The girls had brought some books with them and soon filled the bookcases. The collection was supplemented by paperback editions from Special Service. The library was set up for the use of both patients and hospital personnel. Book carts were taken through the wards twice a week so that books could be borrowed by the bed patients. Evelyn Shieber noted the type of books that were most popular:

"Mystery and Western stories are popular, also a bit scarce. War stories are scorned - the men have had too much of the real thing." - 123rd General Hospital Red Cross Archives.

The Red Cross even managed to obtain a small number of French books for the French patients at Foxley.

Unfortunately both the boxes of craft and card game kits went missing en route from the U.S. to Foxley. Cards and table games were borrowed from a nearby unit to use in the Recreation Hall and in some of the wards. Lois Joseph managed to obtain a piano in London along with craft and games supplies to replace the missing ones. The box of craft materials finally arrived at the camp at the end of August.

In September more easy chairs and writing tables were acquired through Special Service and a large stove was installed. In October the grey concrete floor was painted maroon to give a feeling of warmth to the room and a fireplace was built which made the hall:

Red Cross girls with mobile library at 52nd General Hospital. A similar book cart would have been used at Foxley. (Photo per Mike Webster).

"more homelike and friendly." - 123rd General Hospital Red Cross Archives.

After the installation of the fireplace Evelyn Shieber noted:

"It is a bit difficult to describe the change the fireplace made in the hall except to say that it added an indefinable air of home and it has proven definitely relaxing to patients who are still a bit tense from their battle experiences." - 123rd General Hospital Red Cross Archives.

Isabel Knaus added:

"There is never a time when it is not surrounded by patients relaxing in easy chairs, reading, sleeping or just talking with one another." - 123rd General Hospital Red Cross Archives.

In November 1944 a public address system was installed, 66 loud speakers were situated throughout the hospital. The P.A. was used for broadcasting programmes originating in London (American Forces Network), making announcements about the trips and notifying wards when books and magazines were ready for distribution. It was also used to provide music for dances when the detachment orchestra was unavailable. Personnel of the 123rd took responsibility for the P.A., running request programmes with records and selecting radio programmes to be broadcast. More than 10,000 requests were received but owing to the one-hour per night allotted for this purpose only 2,000 records were played. At Christmas Dickens's Christmas Carol was broadcast through the P.A. system.

In December a large tent was erected between the Chapel and the Recreation Hall. The staff were relieved to be able to move the craft shop to the tent as the small craft room in the office building became crowded with just four patients in it and its proximity to the offices made it almost impossible for the staff to concentrate while the patients were working in the craft shop. The tent was described as having:

 " - *somewhat uneven floors and two stoves that could heat it comfortably even in the coldest weather. Lighting is a bit bad." - 123rd General Hospital Red Cross Archives.*

In April 1945 two additional nissen huts for the use of the Red Cross were erected next to the office building. One hut was to be used as a games room and the other for crafts. The craft hut replaced the tent. The men of the Rehabilitation section of the hospital helped to set up the craft shop in the new nissen hut by building tables and benches. The hut was an improvement on the tent and Isabel Knaus commented:

"The patients seem happy to have a place in which to work without being overcrowded." - 123rd General Hospital Red Cross Archives.

Another nissen hut was erected near the officer patient ward and although this building did not come under the jurisdiction of the Red Cross the girls did assist the Special Service and General Supply in furnishing it. The use of the extra building meant that the Recreation Hall could now become a quiet room for reading, writing and relaxing.

In March 1945 the Red Cross was able to hire one of the medical detachment to clean and upkeep the buildings the Red Cross was responsible for. The girls were also able to take on a civilian employee who was paid for by the British Government to assist in the Recreation Hall. Isabel Knaus described him as:

 " - *a quiet man of 62 years and in poor health so that he cannot do a full time job, but he potters around and does a fair job of keeping the hall in order and the fires going." - 123rd General Hospital Red Cross Archives.*

Also in March the patients and staff of the hospital helped to brighten up the outside of the buildings. A rustic bridge was constructed across the small stream and seats were built around the trees. Bricks were placed edgewise to form borders of flower gardens and daffodils, primroses and other flowers were planted there.

At the beginning movies shown in the detachment day room furnished twice weekly by Special Service provided the only outside entertainment for the men. Later a building was set-aside for this purpose and movies could be shown daily except for Mondays when Officer's Training classes were held. Detachment personnel only were admitted on Wednesdays, Fridays and Sundays, patients were admitted Tuesdays, Thursdays and Saturdays. Twice weekly movies were shown to officers (both staff and patients). Early in October the Red Cross received a movie projector unit, which relieved the pressure on the Special Service unit, which had been carrying out a double duty in showing ward movies in addition to the training and orientation films. The projectionist, who was a member of the medical detachment, was paid $1.25 per day for six days a week.

In 1945 the cinema was improved by the addition of comfortable seats and the construction of a projection booth. A public address system was established within the cinema providing the audience with music before each showing. When the patient numbers dropped towards the middle of 1945 special showings for patients only were discontinued.

The first party held by the Red Cross was just ten days after the unit's arrival:

"Several patients took over the teaching of new card games; others served the refreshments of coffee and cookies. Since the presence of girls always adds fun to any party contacts were made through the military with the Commandant of a nearby W.A.A.F. camp to have eighteen W.A.A.Fs with N.C.O. chaperones attend the latest party. All members of the staff were on hand to guide the party along purely informal lines as regards games and a detachment man came to play the piano for group singing. The serving of refreshments was done by the patients, as was the K.P. work afterwards. Transport for the girls was provided by the hospital. Since this party has turned out so well arrangements have been made with the W.A.A.F. Commandant for bringing her girls here to weekly parties." - 123rd General Hospital Red Cross Archives.

From October the Red Cross held dances for the patients. The first was a Halloween tea dance from three to five p.m. Its setting was the Detachment Day Room:

" - which was festooned with orange and black streamers and cut-outs of black cats, pumpkins and witches. Patients did the decorating under Red Cross supervision. Dancing partners were civilian girls from a nearby town." - 123rd General Hospital Red Cross Archives.

The next dance was held to celebrate Thanksgiving and was held in the Recreation Hall as it was:

"smaller and cozier." - 123rd General Hospital Red Cross Archives.

This dance was held on a Tuesday night, as this was the regular evening for the W.A.A.Fs to visit Foxley. The Red Cross felt that the dance was a great success:

"Needless to say the patients had a wonderful time and clamored for more dances but we felt that we couldn't ask the band to play 'gratis' for more than once monthly." - 123rd General Hospital Red Cross Archives.

The Red Cross Recreation Department was called upon several times to assist in arranging detachment dances for the staff of the hospital. This involved planning decorations and refreshments, obtaining girls and then chaperoning the events.

For the patients confined to wards it was necessary to organise different activities. The four traction wards were given St. Patrick's parties in March 1945. Edna Fecht organised a troupe of guitar and mandolin players and singers who visited the wards bringing with them copies of Irish songs to sing. The Red Cross also organised bingo games, musical quizzes, contests, movies and Red Cross and U.S.O. shows. All birthdays in the wards were recognised with cakes from the hospital bakery. A sketcher from the U.S.O. spent nearly a week at Foxley in February 1945 sketching one patient from each ward that he visited. Evelyn Shieber noted that:

"Great interest was aroused and the rec. workers always knew when he had been in a ward for that was the prime topic of conversation during his visit." - 123rd General Hospital Red Cross Archives.

Also in February the piano was mounted on a trolley so that it could be moved from ward to ward. Evelyn noted that:

" - it has already proved its worth as noted in the case of a listless bed patient whose right leg was in a cast. We learned that he was, or rather is, a pianist, so, as a surprise, we rolled in the piano. He was placed in a wheel chair and brought as close to the piano as was possible in the circumstances. He kept that piano going for three hours. Patients came in from all over and we had an informal song and jam session. He didn't need a sleeping pill afterwards - for the first time since he was brought here - and his apathy disappeared never to return. We left the piano there for some time, only taking it out when it was needed elsewhere. The patients in his ward enjoyed the music so much that they would voluntarily move the instrument back to the ward when our visiting performers had finished with it". - 123rd General Hospital Red Cross Archives.

Crafts could be carried out on the wards when the Recreation workers visited. The men were able to carry out a wide variety of craft activities on the wards including weaving scarves, knotting belts, making raffia slippers for ward use, making leather articles and felt toys. They could also make divisional insignia in petit point. This was a popular activity as a number of the men had lost their insignia and couldn't obtain replacements.

Those patients that could walk could visit the craft shop, which was first situated in a small two by four room in the office building, then in the tent and then in the newly built nissen hut. While in the tent the staff made use of the expertise of one of the patients who had his own contracting business in civilian life:

"Not only did he assist others in their work with metal and wood but he also took the time to build us a much needed cabinet. With his help we kept the shop open several nights a week and invited the detachment, as well as the patients, to use the shop at these times." - 123rd General Hospital Red Cross Archives.

In the craft shop patients could use the tools and materials available to make a variety of items including coin bracelets, pins, rings, billfolds, picture frames, rugs, letter openers, figurines and book ends. The patients could work with metal, leather, plexiglas, raffia or felt. Isabel Knaus found that the craft shop was popular with the patients:

"We have never tried to force craft activities on the patients which is contrary to our policy, but as we have been able to present more and varied types of crafts, more and more patients have become interested and showing a desire to participate." - 123rd General Hospital Red Cross Archives.

In the craft shop the girls held:

"An informal class in clay modeling with patients and rec. worker taking turns in reading instructions on how to make plaques, figurines and ashtrays. The results were a bit crude but everyone had a lot of fun in the doing." - 123rd General Hospital Red Cross Archives.

The girls needed to enlist the help of volunteers from the locality as the 156th had done, so, in November 1944 a 'Volunteer Program' was commenced with the aid of Mrs. Hinckes, the Volunteer Liaison Officer. It was decided to begin with three volunteers, one to serve as a librarian and two others to help with the sewing and repairing of clothes belonging to the patients and staff at the hospital. Edna Fecht remembers that the volunteers were *'a great help'* and that they would also visit the wards with toilet articles and recreation materials as well as taking some of the more routine duties off the shoulders of the Red Cross workers.

The first three ladies to be taken as volunteers were Flora Campbell, Mary Frost and Margaret Mary Dawes. Flora Campbell and Mary Frost left in March 1945 as they had moved away and were not able to get the extra petrol rations needed to travel the extra distance. Two more volunteers, Ruby Palmer and Mrs. Mason were enlisted to take their places. Ruby Palmer supervised musical quizzes and songfests for the patients. In May 1945 more volunteers joined the team. Mrs. Hinckes came to assist the group and Mary Frost was able to return for one afternoon a week to assist in the Rec.Hall. Mrs. Cooke, who was married to an American officer and had been helping out at the A.R.C. Club in Hereford, joined the team at Foxley too. She had a car of her own and a petrol allowance provided by the British Red Cross.

The staff of the American Red Cross at Foxley was keen to foster good community relationships. They had contacts with the British Red Cross who helped, when necessary, to house visiting British friends and relations of patients and also made it possible for patients to attend British Red Cross social events.

In the first couple of months at Foxley the Red Cross were contacted by several organisations that were keen to support its work in raising the morale of the patients. The W.V.S, the Order of St. Golan and the French Society of English Speaking People all offered their services. Free French patients, of which there were a number at Foxley, were visited at the hospital and invited out to tea by the latter group.

In September 1944 Isabel Knaus recorded her intentions regarding the British Red Cross and W.V.S:

"Mindful of the recent directive from Headquarters and also being well aware of their own heavy responsibilities, we have, to date, asked their help in only incidental ways." - 123rd General Hospital Red Cross Archives.

Mr. Williams, of the British Ministry of Information, also offered to send lectures and arrange tours for the patients of the 123rd as well as the 156th. Twice monthly tours were arranged around points of interest, historical or otherwise. A police sergeant usually acted as a guide on these outings. Sunday outings were also arranged for the patients and theatre managers in Hereford opened their matinee performances to groups of patients. It was possible for the patients to visit the Garrison Theatre in Widemarsh Street, the Kemble in Broad Street and Red Hill Hostel.

Civilian girls from the Red Cross Club in Hereford arranged to visit the wards to have Sunday tea with the ambulatory patients in the Recreation Hall. It was necessary for the girls to be chaperoned. A group of school children, along with their teachers, also came to visit the patients in the ward, bringing with them fruit and flowers. A group of small boys from the local area were regular visitors to the wards bringing apples and flowers.

In concluding her March 1945 report Evelyn Shieber writes:

"I would like to say that our contacts with the English have continued to be of the best. They arrange tours, teas and movies for us. We have yet to ask them for something and be turned down." - 123rd General Hospital Red Cross Archives.

The staff at the hospital was also happy to cooperate with the Red Cross. In her report for the end of 1944 Isabel Knaus writes:

We have found that both our working and personal relationships have become more closely knit. - The relationship between the hospital personnel and the Red Cross has always been fine and continues to grow as time goes on. - The medical detachment in the various departments are always most cooperative." - 123rd General Hospital Red Cross Archives.

Evelyn Shieber wrote around the same time:

"Cooperation of the hospital staff has continued to be of great assistance to us in our work. Prior to Christmas one of the workers has asked to speak about the Recreation Program at the meeting of doctors and nurses. She also expressed the staff's appreciation and asked for continued cooperation from the hospital. Since then doctors and nurses alike have been extremely willing to ask for help when they found patients who needed it. This means a lot to the rec. workers for there is so much they find to do that at times they may accidentally overlook some particular case." - 123rd General Hospital Red Cross Archives.

It was necessary for the Red Cross to work closely with the hospital staff. Doctors and nurses would refer any personal or social problems to the Red Cross as they came across them. In some cases staff would refer to the Red Cross if specialised recreation activities or recreation was needed. Most of the casework involved the patients. Isabel Knaus wrote in November 1944:

"Many times our communications regarding a home situation is the first the patient has received in several months and it greatly relieves his mental strain and worry, which, in turn, helps him physically. This often leads him to discuss his problem more freely with us." - 123rd General Hospital Red Cross Archives.

A small percentage of the cases concerned members of the medical detachment, as was the case when Private Roy Thompson was referred to the Red Cross. He was anxious as he hadn't heard from his wife for a couple of months and was worried about her and his child. The Red Cross sent a cable to the wife to find out if there was a problem. Unfortunately when the wife replied it was to ask for a divorce. When Private Thompson received the reply he wanted compassionate leave to return home and see his family. The Red Cross could not grant this unless there was a 'Home Conditions Report, which would involve a Red Cross worker visiting the home and filing a report on it. Private Thompson was reluctant to sanction this as he felt that it would further antagonise his wife. The Red Cross discussed the situation with him and reported:

"We advised we would ask for a home conditions interview and a worker who has understanding and is diplomatic would ask for information on the basis that the serviceman was not clear as to why she wanted a divorce." - 123rd General Hospital Red Cross Archives.

Unfortunately the situation got worse a couple of weeks after the meeting, Private Thompson heard that while his wife had been at work the housekeeper she had employed had left his child alone in a sink. The child had turned on the hot tap and scalded him/herself. The child was hospitalised with third degree burns and the wife was writing to ask for more money to cover the hospital bills. This made Private Thompson even more anxious to go home to see the child and sort out the situation with his wife. Unfortunately the remainder of the case notes are missing so we don't know how the situation was resolved.

The Red Cross provided other miscellaneous services for the patients. After each new convoy of patients the girls would visit the wards, talk to new patients and give out articles such as toothbrushes, toothpaste, cigarettes and matches. They wrote letters, sent cablegrams and money orders home and wrapped and sent home Purple Heart medals and other awards. The staff was also able to make loans to those going on furlough as the army regulation of paying a serviceman one pound five shillings once every two weeks did not cover the expenses incurred while they on furlough.

The Red Cross also helped to find rooms for visitors. They contacted the Red Cross in other hospitals regarding friends and relatives of patients and attempted to locate friends and relatives in other units through the Field Directors. They also mended clothing and ran a shopping service for the bed-ridden patients. The shopping service was increased around October/November 1944 as Christmas came nearer.

Christmas 1944 was a busy time for the Red Cross staff. Isabel Knaus reported that:

"It is our earnest desire not to spare any effort to make this Christmas as happy a one as possible under the circumstances." - 123rd General Hospital Red Cross Archives.

The staff at the hospital was eager to help as much as possible. Several nights each week nurses joined the Red Cross in making and filling stockings and making tree decorations. A box was placed in the P.X. for staff to donate candies, cookies and gum for the patients. Women from two nearby villages also made Christmas stockings to fill with apples and small articles. These were distributed late on Christmas Eve and placed on the bedside tables of each patient along with the Christmas boxes sent from Headquarters.

Fifty trees were purchased from the Davenport Estate by the hospital authorities, tree and ward decorations were made from Christmas wrapping paper, silver paper, tin foil, pinecones and cotton and silver backed paper from the P.X. The nurses, doctors and patients decorated their own wards while the Red Cross Staff decorated the Mess Halls. The best-decorated ward was given a party and a beautifully decorated cake from the mess hall. The judges were two visiting Wrens and Lieutenant Estabrook of the Physiotherapy Department. Christmas murals were painted on the walls of the Recreation Hall by three patients. Using tempera paints the three worked day and night recreating Christmas card scenes of snowy villages. One mural had a small sign saying 'Off Limits to all Military Personnel'.

A number of events were planned for the Christmas season. There were ward parties, a Christmas dance and several U.S.O. shows. Local school children came to carol sing to the patients and in return were given a party in which the patients joined in. Over the Christmas period patients were taken to a local twelfth century church and then invited to tea at a home in Hereford. Half a dozen crutch cases were invited to tea in a Welsh home.

In the week following Christmas the Red Cross staff and the patients played host to fifteen five-year-old evacuees who were quartered in a castle not far from Foxley. The children were taken to visit patients in the wards where they delighted the patients by singing to them. They were rewarded with candy, gum and cookies from the men and as they left were given gifts and sweets.

To celebrate New Years Eve the Red Cross organised a dance. Admission was a paper hat. Later the hats were judged, the winner was the wearer of a pirate hat.

As the war in Europe neared its end Red Cross activities and events were decreased. In April 1945 Frances Thomas, the Staff Aide, was transferred to the 156th General Hospital as it moved to the continent. Isabel Knaus reflected at the time:

"We were extremely sorry to see her go and have felt her loss very much." - 123rd General Hospital Red Cross Archives.

Tom Glennon recalls that Frances Thomas was often on hand to regulate the activities of some of the officers from other groups based at Foxley. Of her attitude towards Colonel Fairchild an officer of one of the artillery groups, who could sometimes get 'out of hand', he states:

"And how the slight and frail girl could order rank about." - The Officers Club - Thomas Glennon.

When Frances left it was necessary for the Red Cross to manage with four staff members until May 17 when Mary Woodward arrived at Foxley. She had not worked in a hospital before but she soon got accustomed to her responsibilities, namely to run the Recreation Hall, and assist in the games room with group activities as well as writing letters for the patients.

As the patient load decreased more patients could get passes into Hereford so the picture show trips were discontinued. Picnic trips were popular as the weather improved. The destination was usually Symonds Yat where softball could be played on the riverbank. The day would be concluded with a trip down the river and tea served on the hillside.

One Sunday in May the Red Cross obtained permission to take patients on a bike hike. Evelyn Shieber reported on the outing:

"The hike was successful if measured by fun, for although we were tired and wet (this English weather) the boys wanted to know about the next one. We were unable to continue the bike hike. Because of a series of accidents on bikes they have been restricted to camp." - 123rd General Hospital Red Cross Archives.

Presumably the medical staff had enough work on their hands dealing with battle injuries without further casualties from bike accidents. Plans for further bike hikes had to be cancelled. Looking back on the year the Red Cross unit spent with the 123rd Evelyn Shieber reflected:

" - our patients tell us that the friendly spirit of the Red Cross staff makes the 123rd General Hospital a place to which they would like to return." - 123rd General Hospital Red Cross Archives.

Chapter 12

RECREATION

Troop morale is an important factor in wartime and can affect the efficiency of an organisation. Lieutenant Richard Penick, Adjutant of the 123rd recognised this and wrote in his report for 1944:

"Morale of this General Hospital was considered high. Officers, patients and enlisted personnel of the Medical Detachment were pleased with the food and housing conditions. For the patients the American Red Cross provided a recreation hall equipped with a ping-pong table, dart games, checker sets and a library containing popular books and current magazines, newspapers and other periodicals. Daily programs were drawn up for the entertainment of hospitalised personnel. Movies were shown at least twice weekly to patient and detachment audiences and several U.S.O. shows were given in the area. Sports equipment was obtained for the use of convalescing patients and for detachment personnel."
- 123rd General Hospital Archives.

The Special Service Section, under the direction of Lieutenant Avery Patton, organised activities for off duty time. Softball and basketball squads were drawn up. There was even a nurse's softball team. Games were scheduled with teams from other hospitals and military installations. Two softball leagues were set up among the departments and clinics.

"This program not only offered each participant additional physical exercise, but likewise served to stress departmental pride and rivalry." - *123rd General Hospital Archives.*

Tom Glennon recalls watching baseball matches involving teams from the 123rd:

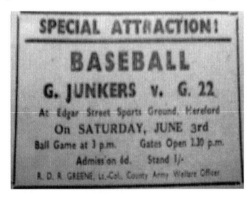

Baseball game involving U.S.Forces advertised in Hereford Times (Hereford Times).

Several officers, including Tom Glennon, spectating at softball game (V.Haines).

"*The good natured banter from those who crowded our sidelines added spice to the game and produced many a laugh and witty remark. The classic remark to all those heard during the long season must have been the one contributed by Sergeant Green on the occasion of Captain Reed's first appearance at the plate. The good-natured Captain had shown a tendency to plumpness, but even so we doubted whether Sergeant Green was justified in asking him the question, 'Who is that man in front of you, Captain?' At the time the batter merely took a hitch in his belt displacing somewhat the extra man, but the question followed him for many months, his golf associates in particular, presenting the query at the most inopportune moments.*" - The Officers Club - Thomas Glennon.

Lieutenant Patton arranged permission for the personnel of the 123rd to use the Ravens Causeway Golf Course, which was situated about five miles away from Foxley by road. It could also be reached cross-country by walking over the hill behind the nurses' quarters, through a field of oats, down a country lane to a narrow road that led to the clubhouse. Tom Glennon remembers:

"*Those who walked - were rewarded with a view beyond compare. Reaching the crown of high land before entering the woods and looking over the rolling landscape as it stretched out below, one had the feeling of being on top of the world and close up against the sky. There was nothing to mar the splendid view, the broad expanse of green broken only by the well marked furrows and snake like roads." - The Officers Club - Thomas Glennon.*

Four sets of golf clubs were left with the managers, Mr. and Mrs. Barnes, two for the use of officers and two for the enlisted men. The fee was very reasonable, being the equivalent of about 30 cents.

The men were made to feel very welcome by Mr. and Mrs. Barnes. For a small sum afternoon tea of sandwiches, cakes and a pot of tea was served. As the couple got to know the men better tea often expanded into dinner or supper with eggs, fried potatoes, vegetables and soft rolls, followed by tea and dessert. Some men were even invited for a full Sunday dinner. When this happened they would take food with them because of the rationing situation. Tom Glennon was under the impression that much of the food served there may have come directly from the mess halls of the 123rd, as it seemed similar to that which was served at the hospital.

Colonel Cherasky often donated food luxuries to the Barnes' table. He was a particularly keen golfer. Tom Glennon comments that:

"Such enthusiasm was displayed by the gentleman in the first days of his interest that some of our officers feared for his army career. - Those of us who followed the Colonel closely knew how high and how low he could travel in spirit during the progress of a game and how often, after a few disastrous holes, he would firmly assert that he was giving up the past time as to that particular moment." - The Officers Club - Thomas Glennon.

This decision never lasted and Colonel Cherasky's enthusiasm for the game meant that Tom, Captain Bloomer and Captain Sutherland could be assured of a lift in the Colonel's jeep to the golf course.

The course at Ravens Causeway was not an easy one. Tom Glennon recalls that:

"Blind holes were numerous and fairways too narrow. - Often we were startled to learn that a ball apparently driven down the center of the fairway had disappeared. A long search would result in failure and a strong feeling of unbelief. On reporting the incident to the manager, Mr. Barnes, we were offered the explanation that the ball either had rolled into a rabbit hole or had been mistaken for an egg and been carried away by a raven or crow." - The Officers Club - Thomas Glennon.

Back at Foxley, soon after the arrival of the 123rd off duty clubs were set up for the enlisted men, non-commisioned officers and officers. Buildings were assigned for their use. The enlisted men had a Detachment Day Room equipped with comfortable chairs, a radio, ping-pong table, games and reading material. About once a month the enlisted men held a dance either in the Day Room or in the Town Hall in Hereford.

Elected officers under the supervision of a Detachment Officer operated the N.C.O. Club. The officers also elected a governing body of directors for the officer's club which was equipped with a bar and lounge and was open each evening until 2400 hours with the exception of Saturdays when closing time was 0200 hours. A firm in Walsall supplied several slot machines for use in the club and this became a welcome source of income to the club until they were banned in 1945. There was an initiation fee of one pound to join the Officer's Club and a monthly charge of ten shillings for membership.

Tom Glennon, known to most affectionately as 'Pappy' managed the Officer's Club. He recalls the problems he encountered in procuring alcohol for the club:

"Improvisation being a strong custom in the army no one could, or should, have been surprised that a beer keg stand and a bar of sorts appeared from nowhere to appease the appetites of spirit thirsty officers and nurses. Hard liquor was rather scarce that first week at Camp Foxley and the manager has a fond recollection of picking up in Hereford his first three bottles of Scotch whisky at the startling price of three pounds ten. Though it was to be a routine price throughout the long months of our stay in England, our officers paid it without a murmur, the impression was always present in our minds that we were treated rather shamelessly considering the reason for being where we were at that time. The shady business, though necessary, had a slight American touch to those familiar with the illegitimate whisky sales of the prohibition era. But the rules of supply and demand still prevailed and whatever our feelings in the matter the fact remains that liquor was vitally necessary to the social life of us all when three thousand miles from our ways of life and living." - The Officers Club - Thomas Glennon.

It was very difficult for Tom to procure sufficient amounts of alcohol to run the club. He found himself having to knock at the side doors of some of the establishments in Hereford and Malvern, buy a few bottles and then hide them in his coat. At one point there was a complaint against one of the establishments that was supplying the club so it was necessary to keep a low profile for a while.

A few weeks after the opening of the club Major Craden of the 93rd General Hospital, based at Blackmore Park, Worcestershire arranged an appointment for Tom with 'Burrow and Company' based in Malvern. It was agreed that Burrow and Company would supply the unit with one case of Scotch whisky each week at the cost of three pounds, seventeen shillings and sixpence per bottle. The firm also agreed to supply soda water, wine and soft drinks.

Other suppliers to the Officers Club were a Mr. Smith from Hereford, who delivered a truckload of beer and other drinks weekly, and a Mr. Hardin from Walsall, who supplied a number of cases of whisky and gin on the black market. At one point Tom agreed to take a case and a half of rum from Mr. Hardin, which he was later to regret. After sampling the rum the men accused the club authorities of trying to poison the members as it was of such poor quality. Once Tom had decided to let the members drink it for free instead of charging three shillings a glass the complaints stopped.

The last source of alcohol for the club was the British Naafi, which Tom believed:

" - had been created by the British for the sole purpose of distributing spirits to officers of American units stationed in England." - The Officers Club - Thomas Glennon.

The Naafi would calculate the unit's allowance by the number on the roster the previous month. The club was allowed to buy one bottle of scotch per five officers and one bottle of gin per ten officers. Tom found this source to be the best for quality and also cheaper at one pound two shillings per bottle. The members paid three shillings per glass for whisky, whatever price had been paid for it wholesale. Often club funds were used to subsidise the price of it.

The officers held a dance each Saturday night at the club while Bingo parties were a regular Wednesday night feature. The first Saturday night party was held in September 1944. Tom remembers:

"The noise-crowded evening was the first of many such parties which were to grace our constantly improving rooms. Ample though our club was for a large crowd, I believe that all of us will ever retain a picture in our minds of a windmilling mass and a constant din as our impression of that first night.

All our repressed feelings of the preceding weeks burst out in gay abandon as the familiar tunes echoed through the low ceilinged rooms. Those we had known only by sight now became our partners on the dance floor or our close companions over the tall glasses. There was truly born the friendships that were to carry us through the long months. There was the foundation of the social life overseas that was to create for us a favourable reputation among the hospitals in the European Theatre of Operations and that was to preserve at a high level the morale among ourselves so necessary to the proper and efficient performance of our duties." - The Officers Club - Thomas Glennon.

Two large stoves and a fireplace were built in the club and the fires were kept going almost constantly through the winter months. Tom recalls:

"The younger, more romantic, members of our group took full advantage of the setting, gathering in pairs to stare at the dancing flames and the glowing coals while they sipped tall glasses of scotch and soda." - The Officers Club - Thomas Glennon.

During the coal shortage early in 1945 fires were forbidden before 5:00 p.m. but:

" - the internal heat obtained by the ingestion of alcohol by our ranks more than offset the deficiency in that room." - The Officers Club - Thomas Glennon.

The Officer's Club opened its doors to officer patients and also officers of the various units that shared Foxley Camp with the 123rd. Tom remembers that members of the other units would often help in cleaning and decorating the club for special occasions like the Halloween Party. In May 1945 the 156th General Hospital's Officer's Club was closed so the 123rd included them in their membership until their departure the following month.

The personnel of the 123rd and 156th also had the opportunity to spend some of their off duty time off base. The two hospital units had arrived at Foxley when the double daylight system was in force, so between supper and bedtime there was ample time to look around the area surrounding the camp. Tom Glennon recalls that one of the first things that the personnel wanted to know when they arrived at Foxley was how far the nearest town was and when they could visit it.

Foxley is situated in a rural part of Herefordshire next to the small village of Mansel Lacy. Mansel Lacy had no village pub but Moorhampton, the next nearest village did. Moorhampton was a small village centred around the train station where the patients arrived in hospital trains. Tom Glennon recalls:

"First reports told of the English 'pub' situated in Moorhampton where one might quench his thirst with a glass of beer or even a scotch and soda. And, of course, one had a picture in his mind of a cozy country inn, quaint and attractive, complete with the rustic simplicity as the period of Sam Weller or Mr. Pickwick and a bartender possessed of sideburns, a bald head and a cockney accent." - The Officers Club - Thomas Glennon.

Tom was unprepared for what actually met him at Moorhampton:

"The town itself burst upon us in a total of four buildings, red brick and rusty, three of them unquestionably dwellings and the fourth resembling more the farmhouse of an extensive farm, which it was, than the tavern of our dreams." - The Officers Club - Thomas Glennon.

Tom and his colleagues ordered a cider and then observed the interior of the pub:

"The small bar seemed no more than a wooden stand and a rail set up in front of a backdrop resembling an open bookcase attached to the wall, in which reposed a limited number of bottles. It was not determined where the beer came from except that it reached the glasses by means of a hand pitcher. It was evidently replenished

Village of Moorhampton 2003 (M.Collins).

in the back room from what, and under what conditions of cleanness we were never able to discover." - The Officers Club - Thomas Glennon.

Tom also noticed that the glasses were washed in a bowl of water that was not renewed during whole evening. Unimpressed with the standards of cleanliness at the pub Tom and his companions chose to investigate the drinking establishments in Hereford situated eight miles from the base and reached by bus. Tom remembers counting fifty-six pubs in Hereford, and while he felt that most of them were superior to the one at Moorhampton he still felt that standards of cleanliness were not high enough. Perhaps this was because he was a dentist by trade.

Other G.Is based at Foxley enjoyed visiting the pubs in Hereford. As Dave Stofer of the 553rd Engineer Heavy Pontoon Bridge Battalion, who was at Foxley in the early part of 1944, recalls:

"We spent a great deal of time in pubs."

He recalls that the pubs were not usually well stocked with whisky, if they had any at all; it would all be of the same brand. He remembers once finding a pub that had whisky and making himself very ill by drinking it to excess. Since then he cannot tolerate the smell of it.

Robert Masterpolo, a patient of the 123rd General Hospital also visited the pubs in Hereford. He remembers that one had a buffet where you picked

Pub at Moorhampton, now a private house 2004 (M.Collins).

out what you wanted and then paid for what you took. He recalls that one of the dishes was fried rabbit. At the end of the evening he discovered that he'd missed the last bus back to Foxley. He was prepared to hike back when the R.A.F. and R.C.A.F. lads in the pub offered him a lift to Credenhill R.A.F. camp (which was halfway to Foxley) in a lorry that was coming to pick them up. When it arrived it was driven by a W.A.A.F. Robert remembers the men singing on the way back:

"This is my story
This is my song
I've been in the Air Force
Too - - - - - - - - long."

On another occasion Bob missed the last bus back to base, a Lieutenant Colonel from Foxley offered to share a taxi back with him. Unfortunately the M.Ps turned up and wouldn't allow it as enlisted men couldn't ride with officers. Bob had to wait for a lift in a truck and was late back. He got let off with a reprimand as he was due to return to his outfit on the continent the next day.

From 1943 G.Is were often to be seen around the city of Hereford. As well as the two hospital plants at Foxley there was a General Hospital at

Barons Cross, Leominster (135th) and an American General Depot at Moreton on Lugg. A number of American artillery units also spent some time training in the Hereford area before being shipped to the continent.

The people of Hereford were curious about the Americans, so in April 1944 the Hereford times published a chart explaining the significance of the various U.S. insignia that G.Is around Hereford were wearing with the following comment:

"Here are a few designs which may help to allay curiosity as to rank or branch of service in the U.S.A. Forces now so pervasive of the British scene." - Hereford Times April 1944.

Ten percent of the 123rd was permitted to visit Hereford nightly and 24 and 48-hour passes were offered periodically. Patient personnel whose health was sufficiently improved were also given passes to visit Hereford and the surrounding area. Day nurses were given one 48-hour pass and one 24-hour pass each month. Mary Casey, a dietician at the 123rd comments that whenever she had a pass she would go into Hereford. On Friday there was a farmer's market where the nurses would trade their cigarette rations for fresh produce.

The Americans were struck by the age of the buildings in Hereford, particularly the cathedral. Tom Glennon describes it as:

"Massive and majestic, one could trace its long history of eight hundred years in the carefully placed stones, the huge buttresses, the towering spire and the beautifully colored glass of its varied windows. It represented all that England was from the time of the Norman Conquest - church and cathedral, the core of English life, the center of power, temporal and ecclesiastical. To us, whose places of antiquity can boast of only two or three centuries, Hereford and its cathedral seemed almost too far back in history to be possible." - The Officers Club - Thomas Glennon.

Cutting from the Hereford Times showing U.S. insignia. April 1944 (Hereford Times).

The Americans also had access to the library in Hereford and in January 1945 a G.I. placed an article in the Hereford times to thank that institution under the heading:

"U.S. Soldier thanks Herefordshire Libraries,

I wish to express my deep appreciation and admiration for the most efficient service, which your library has offered me since my very recent enquiry concerning reference books for a medieval history course, which I am taking. The opportunity seldom offers itself for one to be associated with an institution, which goes to such great pains in order to thoroughly satisfy. The books, which you have posted to me, have been valuable as a source material and reference books; they are definitely of great use to me. Thank you very much." - Hereford Times 27.01.45.

The G.Is visiting Hereford also attended dances and concerts at the Shire Hall and Town Hall. The Hereford Times reports that in February 1944 a choir of American 'coloured' soldiers was a feature of an evening's entertainment at the Shire Hall in aid of Army Welfare funds. In July an 86 piece American band played on Castle Green for the people of Hereford's entertainment.

The cinema was another source of entertainment in Hereford. The city had four cinemas: the Odeon; the Kemble; (both of which have been demolished) the Ritz (which has now become the Odeon); and the Palladium (known as the 'Flea Pit' and now used as a Bingo Hall). Dave Stofer and

Lacer and Carl McDaniel from 279th Station Hospital (Abergavenny), relaxing by the River Wye in Hereford (C.McDaniel).

Variety Concert at Shire Hall February 1945 (Hereford Times).

Shire Hall 2004 (M.Collins).

The Palladium, now a
Bingo Hall, 2004 (M.Collins).

The Ritz, now the Odeon. 2004
(M.Collins).

Robert Masterpolo both remember being surprised that the English allowed smoking in their cinemas, as in America it was banned. Robert recalls:

"It seemed strange to me to see smoke rising into the light from the projector"

The personnel of the 123rd were also able to enjoy the countryside around Hereford. Tom Glennon remembers cycling with Colonel Sullivan, Major Clift and Captain Ostrand around the country roads beyond Moorhampton, ending the ride with a 'blackberry party'. Tom also remembers enjoying a cycle ride to the Welsh borders and back. At the time he was dressed in O.Ds - (Olive Drab work clothes), although normal dress off base should have been Class A Dress uniform. He was startled to come face to face with the C.O, Colonel McDonald, as he approached Kington. The Colonel stopped him but let him

Hereford Town Hall 2004
(M.Collins).

continue after he had explained the reason for his casual dress.

Lieutenant Patton, the Special Service Officer, would often organise trips off base to places of interest. Each Saturday a trip to Stratford Upon Avon was organised. A truck left the camp at 1:00 p.m. and arrived in Stratford at about 3:30 allowing everyone to visit the historical places like Ann Hathaway's cottage and Shakespeare's house and garden before attending a play at the Memorial theatre. Tom Glennon, who made the trip several times, remembers that sometimes they didn't arrive back until 3:00 a.m. on Sunday morning. Mary Zeller (nee Casey), a nurse with the 123rd, remembers visiting Stratford in March 1945 on a 72 hour pass with her colleague, Lieutenant Harriet Goodman. They saw 'Much Ado About Nothing' at the Memorial Theatre.

In 1945 it was possible for the personnel to use a bus formerly employed on patient tours. This meant that that more people could be transported than previously. Later, Tom found out that Colonel McDonald and Colonel Cherasky had turned a blind eye in allowing the trips as the directive that allowed group transportation limited the distance to fifty miles, while Stratford was at least sixty miles from Foxley.

Cinema listing for the Odeon.
1944 (Hereford Times).

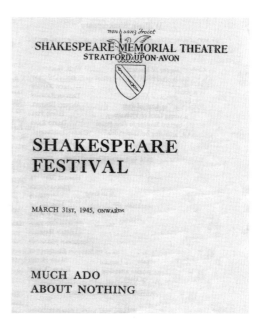

Programme for Shakespeare Memorial
Theatre 1945 (M. Zeller).

Chapter 13
ANGLO-AMERICAN RELATIONSHIPS

A number of the personnel from Foxley were invited to spend some of their off-duty time with English families around the Foxley area. The families contacted the American Red Cross who passed on the invitation to the members of the units. Mary Casey, a dietician with the 123rd who was lucky enough to be given such an invitation, comments about the local British people:

"The people were very hospitable even though their times were desperate. However they were more than willing to share"

When invited to an English home the Americans would often take rations with them – canned meat, vegetables and fruit, to share with the families.

Mary and one of her colleagues were invited to the home of a wealthy businessman. She recalls enjoying the time at his home:

"He took us down to the big seaport of Bristol. We got to see the huge ships in dock - ships with flags from all over the world. He toured us through the town and also took us to his office - He had a huge home and several servants. I remember one of the maids drew my bath water. After drawing my bath water she asked if I wanted my back washed - I had never been treated with such pampering."

The Delahays, an English family, often played host to Pfc. Jerome Morris, who was with the 123rd. Charles Delahay met Jerome at Hay on Wye Train Station where Charles was Stationmaster. When Jerome told Charles how much he missed his home and family Charles invited him to his home to meet his wife and three daughters. One of the daughters, Marjorie, recalls that Jerome enjoyed pony trekking on the Black Mountains with her and her sisters. Jerome never forgot the kindness the family had shown him. After the war they kept in touch and Jerome came over to visit the family several times.

Staff Sergeant Michael Petkas of the 123rd was often invited to the home of Edward Spencer, one of the electricians at the camp. The Spencers lived in

Left - 198 Belmont Road (V. Haines).
Right - Pamela Whiting with Tom Glennon (V. Haines).

Chestnut Drive, Hinton and Michael got married from the house. Edward's daughter, Doreen, remembers that Michael left the wedding cake for the family to finish off and comments:

"I've never seen or tasted anything like it since"

Michael made Doreen and her mother bracelets with their names twisted into them as a thank you gift.

Captain Tom Glennon was invited to stay with the Whitings at Belmont Road in Hereford. Pamela, the teenage daughter of the family was most put out when she was asked to move into the box room so that the American could have the 'best bedroom'. The family were very grateful for the food parcel that Tom's family sent for them while he was staying with them.

The G.Is were keen to repay the citizens of Hereford for the kindness and hospitality they received. For Christmas 1944 the American Red Cross Club entertained a large group of children in the Club building. This was reported in the Hereford Times:

"Santa CLA-US

Hereford children fetched by Americans at their club.

One of the highlights of the Christmas tide was the entertainment given at the A.R.C. Club, Broad Street, to between 60 and 70 Hereford Children on Christmas Day afternoon. The authorities had requested the City Education Authorities to select as far as possible children whose fathers had lost their lives in the war and this request was complied with.

The children, whose ages ranged between four and seven, feasted themselves until they could eat no more, on turkey sandwiches, cookies, cakes, pies, apples, candies and malted milk and were then taken into the big lounge for the playing of games. There were tugs of war with G.Is acting as captains and one of the G.Is later appeared as Father Christmas giving each child a package shipped over from the States by the Junior American Red Cross. These packages contained a variety of gifts that had been packed by American school children whose names appeared on the enclosed greetings card, and through this medium the English recipients will get into contact with their counterparts across the Atlantic. Also on leaving each child was given apples and candies.

The staff and volunteers worked hard to make the party what it was, a grand success and something that will go far towards increasing the already warm relations between us and our great hearted American allies." - Hereford Times 30.12.44.

On Boxing Day another party was given for the children of the club staff.

Earlier in the year the Hereford times had reported on an occurrence involving some children that wasn't so pleasant. This was reported under the headline:

"Abused Kindness

Boy's theft from American soldiers.

'The real fact is that they are very kind to us and we are abusing their kindness', commented Mrs. F.H.B. marsh during the hearing of a case in which five boys were summoned for stealing cigarettes and other articles from the quarters of some American soldiers. The boys complained that the Americans encouraged the boys to fetch beer and sit down and play cards with them. On the other hand the Deputy Chief Constable Mr. G.T. Brierley said that when the Americans first came they were very kind to the children, giving them sweets and so on but the boys and girls took such advantage of this that the Commanding Officer had to make representations and he (Mr. Brierley) had to send police to clear them out of the soldier's quarters, not wishing to do this themselves because they wanted to be friendly. Two brothers aged 12 and 13 and another boy were summoned for stealing cigars, cigarettes and sweets worth £1.14s.4d, the younger brother and the 16 year old being also summoned for stealing a cigarette lighter valued at 5 shillings.

Stick 'Em Up.

After the deputy chief Constable had outlined the case Private G. Clent, U.S. Army, gave evidence of going to his quarters on 20 February and surprising two boys there who ran away. Then he discovered a third hiding behind some clothes hung on a peg. This boy pointed a finger at the witness and said, 'Stick 'em up.' After being searched they found cigarettes, candy and cigars on him. He was taken to an officer and detained until the police arrived." - Hereford Times 11.03.44

The boys were put on probation.

Another offence often reported in the Hereford Times and involving G.Is was 'sleeping out'. This offence seemed to involve girls sleeping outside late at night when there was no reason for them not to be at home. More often than not they were caught sleeping with a man. Reports in the Hereford Times suggest that these girls usually slept with Americans.

In January 1945 Joan Smithers and Irene Imogen Bithel were sent to prison for seven days because they were found:

"Sleeping with American soldiers in a shed" - Hereford Times 27.01.45.
The two girls pleaded guilty to:

" - persistently wandering abroad, not withstanding that a place of shelter is reasonably accessible. - The chairman giving the Bench's decision said a stop must be put to the practice of 'sleeping out' by girls." - Hereford Times 27.01.45.

In March there was a similar case when 23 year old Sylvia Vera Flowers and Ivy Williams pleaded guilty to:

"wandering abroad and sleeping in an air raid shelter off Commercial Road." - Hereford Times 31.03.45.

Both girls had only just been released from prison where they had been sent for being on war property (Flowers) and larceny (Williams).

"The chairman (Mrs. Tomlinson) said that in view of their record and their evading their responsibility of helping their country in wartime the Bench had no option but to send the defendants to prison for three months." - Hereford Times 31.03.45

Three months later Flowers was arrested again for 'sleeping out' near the riverbank and was returned to prison for a further three months.

In April two more women were arrested for this offence. This time one defendant, Dorothy Owens, aged 22 was a married woman with two children. She and Ellen Downs, aged 41 were:

"charged with wandering abroad notwithstanding that a place of shelter was reasonably accessible. They were found with two Americans in a cheese house at Tupsley Court Farm, Hereford at 1:00 a.m." - Hereford Times 02.04.45.

Apparently Owens and a girl she shared a house with had already had five of their children removed from the house by the authorities because of the conduct of the American soldiers who were visiting the premises. In her defence Owens told the magistrates that her husband was no better than she was, but she was still sent to prison for two months while Downs was sent down for a month. After the prison sentence Owens was to return to live with her father who said that:

"His daughter's conduct with other men was causing him a great deal of anxiety." - Hereford Times 02.04.45.

A similar case was brought against unmarried mother, 23 year old Daisy Constance, who was found guilty of neglecting her three children aged between four months and six years. She was found late at night in the company of

American soldiers. Apparently she had been a great source of trouble to her parents as she seemed to have no self-control and wouldn't look after her children, who she left with her parents. As the prosecutor stated:

"She seemed to be one of those who must always be out and had enjoyed herself with soldiers of all descriptions." - Hereford Times May 1945.

Apparently she had come to P.C. Barker's notice on many occasions:

"especially when coloured troops were in the district." - Hereford Times May 1945.

In February 1945 a case was brought against a younger girl whose mother:

" - had admitted that she was unable to control her and she had herself to go out to work." - Hereford Times 10.02.1945.

The girl had apparently stayed out until 12:00 on one night, then spent a second night in a premises in Hereford occupied by an American Services Unit (possibly this was the American Red Cross Club in Broad Street). The American authorities had already taken action against the soldier who had taken her there.

She was found work at a hotel but soon afterwards the management reported that she was still staying out late and on one occasion had got back into the hotel through a window at 1:15 a.m.

"Miss Kell, the Probation Officer, said that she wished to emphasise the fact that the girl was in moral danger and to ask that she be placed in strict discipline." - Hereford Times 10.02.1945.

An application was made to the Education Authority with a view to her being placed in a training home.

The Hereford Times also reports on a U.S. soldier having to face the court for an offence committed in Hereford. On December 16 1944 there was a court martial of a G.I. for assault.

"U.S. Court Martial
Soldier sentenced to five years at Hereford.

At an American General Court Martial held at the Hereford magistrates court on Tuesday Private Floyd le Harness, U.S. Army, was charged with violation of the 93rd Article of War, the specification being that he did, with intent to commit a felony, commit an assault on Violet Frances Slann. Major Albert N. Whitman was the President and sitting with him were three other majors, three Captains and one 1st Lieutenant. The Trial Judge Advocate was Captain Stanley P. Arnell and Captain Nelson G. Waldenburg appeared for the defendant and pleaded not guilty.
Girl's Evidence

Miss Slann of 84 Ross Road, Hereford, said she was going home with her sister when they were stopped by two American soldiers, one of whom was the Accused. He asked her for a date and she arranged to see the Accused at 6:00 on Sunday evening. Her sister declined to go. On the Sunday the Accused called at her house with another soldier but her sister would not go with them. She therefore went with the accused, who she knew as Bob, to the Race Horse Inn where she stayed until closing time. She had two ciders and some other stuff, the accused had some beer. On leaving the pub they went down to the river into a field and sat on the grass. The Accused kissed her and then the alleged assault occurred." - Hereford Times 16.12. 1944.

Private LeHarness was found guilty and was sent to prison with hard labour for five years. He was also dishonourably discharged from the army and lost all pay and allowances that were due to him.

On a happier note the Hereford Times also had more pleasant occasions to report on. A number of weddings took place in Hereford between G.Is and local girls. In June 1945 Corporal Robert Froelik from the 123rd Medical Detachment married Lilian Preece at All Saints Church in Hereford. Lilian wore a white lace dress and white veil held in place by an orange blossom coronet. The bridesmaids, Lilian's sister, Eileen and her friend, Joyce Bryon, wore white organdie with pink trimmings and headdresses of silver leaves. Lilian was also attended by her cousin who wore green satin with a pink veil and headdress and by her nephew, Carfield Davies. Roger's best man was Corporal Robert Hederman, also of the 123rd.

In May 1945 one of the patients of the 123rd was married. The reception was held on the ward at Foxley among his friends. The nurses and chaplain managed to arrange a tiered cake, punch, sweets and flowers.

Wedding photos involving G.Is and local girls from the Hereford Times 1944-1945.

In February 1945 the Hereford Times reported on a wedding between a Hereford bride and U.S. soldier bridegroom who could have come from Foxley. For security reasons the newspaper does not mention the name of the military hospital he served at.

"Hereford Bride - U.S. soldier Bridegroom

Eileen Maud Marston of Hereford and Mr. Chester L. Rossey, serving in the U.S. Army, Warren, Pennsylvania.

The ceremony in Hereford Register Office was followed by a service conducted by a U.S. Army Chaplain at the chapel of the Military Hospital where the bridegroom is stationed in the West of England. The bride wore a white lace gown and veil and coronet of orange blossom, she carried a bouquet of pink carnations and ferns. The bridesmaid, Norah Marston, wore a dress of green lace with mauve accessories and a mixed posy. Private Brown, of the U.S. Army was the best man. The Reception was at the Mitre Hotel, they left for a honeymoon in Birmingham, the bride travelling in a pink crepe dress with oatmeal coloured jigger coat." -
Hereford Times February 1945.

Chapter 14

THE FINAL CHAPTER
OF THE 123RD

On 16 March 1945 the 1363rd Labor Supervision Company, commanded by Captain Halend W.Hankel, arrived at Camp Foxley to prepare a stockade for German Prisoners of War. The M.Ps took over the Manor House while its front lawn became an enclosed prison yard surrounded by high fences of barbed wire and overlooked by a tall wooden tower. The Prisoners of War were to be employed in the two hospitals. On 26 March 125 prisoners began work at the 123rd General Hospital.

The prisoners were employed as labourers to keep the area clean and to improve its landscaping. Mary Zeller remembers that while painting the chapel they painted a swastika on the ceiling. They were made to paint over it, but its outline could still clearly be seen. Some prisoners were employed in the mess halls; they would wash dishes, and sometimes cook. Nurse, Beverley Wilbert, remembers passing a prisoner in the mess hall and muttering to her colleague:

"It's a good job they don't speak English. I'd like to kick him up the rear."
The German turned round and said:

"Fraulein, I do speak English."
At this Beverley made a hasty exit.

On the whole the officers were satisfied with the attitude of the prisoners. The Adjutant, Richard Penick, reported on the prisoners' conduct and work:

"The work accomplished by these prisoners has been considered highly satisfactory and relatively few discipline problems have been encountered." - 123rd General Hospital Archives.

From the beginning of 1945 a policy of replacing general servicemen with limited assignment men had been followed at the hospital. This meant that non-specialist personnel from the Medical Detachment were transferred to the 12th Reinforcement Depot at Tidworth for infantry training and ultimately sent to the continent to replace the wounded men they had been caring for in the hospitals at Foxley. Rehabilitated patients whose disabilities

Tree at Foxley with name of P.O.W. cut into it.

were too severe for them to return to the front, but were not severe enough for them to return home, were assigned to non-combatant jobs that their disabilities would allow them to carry out. Some men who had been declared unfit to return to combat after being wounded were transferred to the hospital staff while badly wounded men were returned home to the U.S.A.

As the end of the war in Europe came nearer the patient numbers of the 123rd decreased. Some wards were closed and 13 members of the 123rd Medical Detachment who had been ward attendants were transferred to the 1363rd Labor Supervision Company to act as guards and interpreters. The patients' mess hall was closed and meals were served on the remaining wards.

On 8 May the Rehabilitation Section was closed and the last group of patients was transferred to the 10th Reinforcement Depot at Lichfield, Staffordshire. The Rehabilitation Staff continued to conduct a physical training programme and classes for ambulatory patients from the medical and surgical wards remaining open. Exercises for bed patients were given twice daily through the public address system by personnel of the Rehabilitation Section.

Also on 8 May V.E. Day was celebrated by the personnel at the hospital with a 48 hour pass. Some of the staff attached this to furloughs that were due to them, to create a longer holiday. Some spent the day in the city of Hereford where the celebrations were reported by the Hereford Times:

"There was, quite justifiably, considerate boisterousness towards the end of the day but everything passed off without any disorderly scenes despite the fact that considerable inroads were made on the special stocks of liquor laid on by the locals.

The big moment of the afternoon, of course, should have been Mr. Churchill's speech, but unfortunately a technical hitch caused by children thronging onto the bandstand and interfering with the wiring of the loudspeakers made it impossible for the eagerly waiting crowd to hear the historical announcement. The Prime Minister's voice could be heard faintly in the immediate vicinity of the bandstand but the purport of his words were known and concluded among cheers." - Hereford Times 12.05.45.

Some of the streets of Hereford held street parties. Mr. and Mrs. J.E. Cheney of the Golden Lion in Berrington Street were the main instigators of the Berrington Street party, although they:

" - received open handed support from their patrons, local tradesmen and from the Americans at Foxley who sent along sweets for the children and the ladies of Hereford American Red Cross Club who provided some more food." - V.E. Day Celebrations in Hereford. - Hereford Times 12.05.45.

In the evening the cathedral was floodlit and American Servicemen were among the public who attended the thanksgiving service there. All four of the Hereford cinemas showed special features during the day.

After V.E. Day some hospitals were alerted for redeployment to the Pacific where hostilities were ongoing. The 156th General hospital at Foxley and the 81st General Hospital at Plant 4183, Rhydlafar, Wales, sent their patients to the 123rd when they were alerted for redeployment.

Also after V.E. Day;

"A liberal leave and furlough policy was adopted, affording all personnel the opportunity to take a seven day leave, during which time any point in the United Kingdom could be visited easily. On 22 June 1945 orders were issued giving 13 enlisted men seven day furloughs to Paris, France, plus three days travelling time. Plans to send additional groups to Paris were altered by the issuance of an order cancelling such leaves owing to lack of transportation." - 123rd General Hospital Archives.

V.E. Day Celebrations in Hereford (Hereford Times 12.05.1945).

On the initiation of the Army Information and Education Programme the hospital began to send small groups of men to Army I. and E. schools. On 10 June 23 officers, including nurses, and six enlisted men were sent to the 6819th Army I. and E. school at Swindon. Following the return of the officers and enlisted men the Army I. and E. Section of the 123rd was expanded and the staff was assigned a complete building formerly used as a ward. Plans were made to establish the military equivalent of a high school within the unit and a survey of qualified instructors was made.

During the last two weeks of June the library was moved from the enlisted Men's Day Room to the former Red Cross Recreation Hall, which was no longer in use, and placed under the supervision of Mariana Thurber of the Special Services Library Branch, who was temporarily assigned to the unit. Two enlisted men of the Medical Detachment were assigned as library assistants. At this point the library held 1,200 hard back and 600 paperback books, fiction and non-fiction as well as magazines.

On 24 June the 123rd received orders to prepare for redeployment overseas. As the 156th had had the same orders a month earlier the 123rd observed their procedures to:

" - *acquire knowledge of the necessary requirement to prepare for such a movement."* - *123rd General Hospital Archives.*

It was necessary to delay the Army I. and E. programmes in order to permit the unit to comply with the training schedule formulated by United Kingdom Base Headquarters for units which are to be redeployed.

In June three medical officers, 1st Lieutenant Richard Michtom, Captain Wylie Griffith and Captain Thomas Quigley had been selected to attend a two-week course at the Medical Field Service School at Les Marais, France. The reason for this course was to prepare the personnel for Pacific duty. It included learning about tropical diseases and shooting a carbine and 45 pistol.

Redeployment classes were prepared on a 15 hour weekly basic to be extended over a four week period. Two groups were formed, one to take place each morning for four hours and the other to take place in the afternoons. The purpose of these classes was to train the personnel for working in the Pacific Theatre of Operations now that the conflict in Europe had been resolved. Propaganda films like 'Two Down and One to Go' and 'On to Tokyo' were shown during these sessions. Full attendance of the sessions was achieved.

Orientation classes were also held each week at the 123rd with group leaders conducting panels and discussions on current topics like: organised

Robert Michtom, Wylie Griffiths and Thomas Quigley on Detached Duty at Medical Field School in France (Robert Michtom).

labour; Japan's aims and philosophies; the war in the Pacific; our Russian allies; and the race question.

By the end of June only four wards were open at Foxley, housing 33 patients. On 4 July the order was received to close the Medical Department. At this point there were just eight patients left. Three were sent back to duty and the other five were transferred to another hospital. After the patients were transferred the surgical service wards were cleaned and all equipment placed in the store room. The enlisted men of the Surgical Department oiled and wrapped instruments which were to be returned.

On 6 July United States Hospital Plant 4179 was officially closed and all departments and clinics began turning in supplies and equipment. The supply department organised the assembly of equipment, ensured that impedimenta was returned to the proper depots, issued and received clothes, crated supplies and equipment.

The British Officer in Charge of Barracks was notified that the Hospital Site was due to be closed. All of the British issued supplies were to remain on post to be checked by a British Representative. A survey of all buildings was taken, checking damage and collecting surplus equipment to see what could be salvaged. Much of the equipment was taken to the G. Depot at

Wylie Griffiths and Thomas Quigley with two French ladies.

Moreton on Lugg, excess chemical warfare was taken to G.25 at Ashchurch, Gloucestershire.

Some equipment was given to the British Hospitals in the area for their use. The Hereford Times announced in August:

"With the end of the war in Europe and the constant reduction of American hospital services in this country some of our own hospitals have been recipients of windfalls from our American friends in the form of equipment of the utmost value, particularly in these difficult times.

The Herefordshire County Council members were acquainted by Captain L.H. Green, who is chairman of the County Council Hospital Committee, of the fact that during the past few weeks the hospital had received two magnificent gifts, one from the American Hospital at Leominster and the other from the American Hospital at Foxley. - They were, said Captain Green, gifts of very considerable value and he wanted publicly to thank the American authorities for their generosity to draw attention not only to their value but the feeling that had prompted the people of the United States who had been running their hospitals in this country to make them. It was evidence of that spirit which all hoped would continue, a spirit developed during the war which they hoped would endure for generations to come." - Hereford Times 4.08.45.

When the Officers Club closed the committee decided to donate their remaining pieces of china to the local regiment in Hereford. Apparently on receipt of the china the regiment placed a plaque on the wall acknowledging the gift to be from the 123rd General Hospital. Tom Glennon comments:

"and though some of our members rebelled at giving anything to the British, it seems now that our policy, kindness and generosity was far more noble than the policy of other units which caused much valuable equipment to be destroyed rather than give the British the benefit of its use." Officers Club - Thomas Glennon.

On notice of the hospital's closure the Headquarters Department was responsible for bringing the personnel records of all the assigned officers and enlisted men up to date.

"This process took four men approximately nine hours per day for eight days, interviewing each enlisted man in the organisation. - Identification tags and cards also were checked during the interview and those which were lost were listed and ordered. - The interviewing team consisted of four men. Each officer was also called into the Personnel Office and interviewed." - 123rd General Hospital Archives.

Following the announcement of the point system for discharge a survey of service records was made and it was found that eight officers and sixteen enlisted men had accumulated more than the prescribed 85 point interim score although three officers and three enlisted men elected to remain in the army until V.J. Day. All men over 39 years of age and those with a score of 75 points or above were transferred out of the unit. All married nurses and the six recently assigned to the unit were assigned to another hospital. 25 nurses were transferred into the organisation.

On 17 July Major Stephen I. Gaull, Headquarters U.K. Base, headed a team that conducted an inspection of the organisation and area. All records, barracks and areas were inspected thoroughly. On 20 July smallpox vaccine was administered to all personnel. The civilian employees were released on 21 July.

To everyone's relief in August the war in Japan ended and the personnel of the 123rd were no longer required to redeploy to the Pacific. Robert Michtom and a forward party were already sailing towards the Pacific at this point. Robert had left London on the day of the announcement of Churchill's defeat in Parliament. Two days away from Gibraltar the ship was turned around and sent to Virginia in the U.S.A.

The remainder of the personnel were returned to the U.S. where most of them received a thirty day furlough. Unfortunately one member of the unit ended up making three trips across the Atlantic. When Patty, Colonel McDonald's dog, arrived at the Port in the U.S. there was no one there to receive her so she was carried back to England and then back to America again, where this time she was returned to her rightful owner.

Around the end of September the personnel of the 123rd met up at Camp Sibert, Alabama, for deactivation of the unit. At this time there was a rule that stated that any money remaining in club funds on deactivation of a unit was to be sent to Washington D.C. Accordingly it was decided that the money in the Officer's Club Fund would be better spent in Alabama on the officers who contributed it. A meal of fried chicken was organised in the ballroom of the Reich Hotel for 110 people.

Alcohol was not easily obtained at the time as Alabama was a 'dry State' except for a number of controlled liquor stores. It was necessary for the officers to collect a number of ration cards from the personnel and then drive around the three liquor stores in the city of Birmingham, returning to one in disguise, to obtain 48 bottles of assorted spirits. Tom Glennon comments that:

"A great effort was made to so arrange the expenditure that only a token would find its way to the coffers of the custodian of funds. How well we succeeded can be judged from the fact that on the day of deactivation your treasurer made out a check of $9.75 payable to Custodian of funds, Washington D.C., which amount represented the balance remaining." - The Officers Club - Thomas Glennon.

The party was enjoyed by all. Colonel McDonald took the opportunity to thank:

"the assembled members for their loyalty and cooperation during the life of the organisation and bid God Speed to them in a visible show of emotion. - Group singing of Auld Lang Sine marked a fitting close to a memorable evening, the last official meeting of the officers of the 123rd General Hospital." - The Officers Club - Thomas Glennon.

Looking back on his time at Foxley, Tom Glennon recalls:

"The memory of thousands who passed through our hospital wards between battlefield and home gives now a pleasing satisfaction to us in having been part of the united effort which ultimately replaced with peace and quiet, the violence of the years of war. Each one of us to the end of his days will recall the incidents of hospital life in England, what was drab, what was difficult and uncomfortable will be covered with the slight forgetfulness that time always effects, what was heartening and good and helpful will stand out stronger in the sweet thoughts of recollection." The Officers Club - Thomas Glennon.

Chapter 15
POLISH REFUGEE CAMP

After the 123rd General Hospital had left Foxley at the end of the war, the camp was used to house the families of Poles who had fought alongside the British in World War Two. Many of the Poles housed at Foxley had fascinating stories to tell about their lives since first leaving Poland at the beginning of the war.

The Second World War for Britain began with Germany's invasion of Poland in 1939. The Polish fought the invaders back through September 1939 but on 17 September Germany's ally, the U.S.S.R, invaded Poland from the East. The Polish President, government and Supreme G.H.Q. were forced to cross the border into Romania, where they were interned. The Polish Campaign had lasted six weeks with high losses to all armies involved.

Bed bases outside huts at Foxley 1946 (M.Maczka).

The U.S.S.R. moved in to occupy much of Poland and many of the Poles were deported to work camps in Siberia. Mr. Marian Maczka and his family were deported from Marian's birthplace in Poland to Siberia by the Russians in 1940. Marian remembers the occasion clearly. On 10 February the family was awakened at 4:00 a.m. by Russians with machine guns and told to report to County Hall, fifteen miles away in Brody. The family were not allowed to pack and were never to see their home again. Eleven-year-old Marian; his

Captain William Hawker, British Officer at Camp Foxley
(H. Pavlovich).

father, who was in his sixties; his mother and his brother and sisters had to travel in a horse drawn sledge through the snow to the County Hall. From there the family was transported in cattle trucks to Archangel, near the Arctic Circle. The thousand-mile journey took two to three weeks. Archangel was a bleak part of Siberia where the land was covered in ice and snow for three quarters of the year.

On arrival the family was split up and placed in different work camps. In the work camps the Russians only required people who were strong enough to carry out manual labour. Marian remembers that well-educated people, like doctors, were executed. The camps consisted of huge squares cut out of forest, miles from any towns or villages. Wild animals roamed the forest and Marian was always nervous if he had to walk through the forest to deliver items to the other camp eight miles away.

On 22 June 1941 Germany invaded the U.S.S.R., therefore the U.S.S.R. joined the Allied Forces against Germany. On 30 July the Polish Government in London signed the Polish-Soviet Agreement, which led to the release of deportees. A Polish Army was formed in Uzbekistan to fight alongside the Russians. Marian's brother, Florian, was one of the men forced to fight with the Russians. Not surprisingly, many Poles did not want to fight alongside the Russians so they crossed the border to Persia and Iraq where British Forces were based. At this point women and children were sent to camps in Africa. Marian's parents and younger sister, Krysia went to a camp in Kenya while Marian's other sister joined the 318th Women's Military Transport Company. In 1942 Marian, who was now 14, joined the Polish Cadet Force, which came under the jurisdiction of the British Army. Here he learnt trades, which were to stand him in good stead in later life.

Christmas dinner for Polish troops in Foxley Mess (H.Pavlovich).

Marian Maczka at Foxley (M. Maczka).

Marian's unit, the 458th Motorised Workshop, followed the Polish 2nd Corps in its campaign through Egypt and Italy. The unit supplied and repaired equipment for the 2nd Corps. Members of the unit, including Marian, entertained the troops. The 2nd Corps finished the war in the Ancona area of Italy and was billeted in Porto San Giorgio for a time. After

Celebrations of Father Ernest Choweuic's
20th Anniversary as a priest (Mrs. Nowasielski).

Corpus Christi Procession at Foxley 1955 (Mrs. Nowasielski).

this they travelled across Italy to set sail from Naples, sailing to the U.K. via Gibraltar. The remainder of Marian's family travelled from Kenya in 1948 to a camp at Wheaton Aston in Staffordshire.

Once in England Marian was assigned to a military barracks in Friar Street, near Hereford Cathedral. He was given guard duty here, for which he was paid one shilling a week. He remembers always being hungry and looking forward to 6:00 p.m. when he would be able to buy a cup of tea and cake from the Naafi for 1d.

The H.Q. for the Polish troops was at Foxley and Marian would often have to report there to get his orders for the day. He was sometimes sent out to work on farms in the area. Once he slipped as he was getting into a truck at Foxley and broke his leg. He was taken to the sick bay at Foxley but unfortunately it didn't have the facilities to deal with his injury so he was sent to the former American hospital that had now become a Polish hospital, at Barons Cross, Leominster He spent six weeks there.

When he reported back to duty at Foxley Marian was given a push-bike and put back to work as a general errand boy. Not long afterwards he was cycling along one of the narrow roads around Foxley when a truck came along on the wrong side of the road and hit him. Marian damaged his knee and had to spend another five weeks at Baron's Cross Hospital. In 1947 Marian was discharged from the Military Forces at Oulton Park, Cheshire.

Tadeusz Michalak, who had also fought in the Polish 2nd Corps and finished the war in the Ancona area of Italy, and his wife, Maria had commenced their journey across Italy in June 1946. They set sail from Naples on 10th August aboard The Empress of Australia arriving at Liverpool on 17 August. From Liverpool they were sent to Wynnstay Camp., situated just outside Ruabon in North Wales and known as Transit Camp Number 81. From this camp they were sent to Foxley.

Mrs. Nowasielski, who also became a resident of Foxley, had a similar history. She was also deported from Poland in 1940 and her family spent some time in Tehran, Persia. Like many of the women and children she was sent to Tanzania until the end of the war. On 1 April 1948 a British transport plane flew her from Nairobi to a holding camp in Cirencester. She was married at this camp to a man she met there who she knew from before the war. Unfortunately he died before their first child was born.

In September 1949 she moved with her baby to Foxley to stay with

Pavlovich family outside Number 398 (H.Pavlovich).

3 Pavlovich children, living accommodation in background (H.Pavlovich).

her parents who had made their home there. Her parents hung a blanket down the middle of the hut they were living in in lieu of a dividing wall to give her some privacy. In 1950 Mrs. Nowasielski moved to a one bedroomed flat in the camp, which had a kitchen, toilet and a sitting room. She remarried while at Foxley and when her second child was born moved into a two bedroomed flat.

Pavlovich children playing in ruins of hut (H. Pavlovich).

Mrs Nowasielski remembers that life in the camp was very much the life of a Polish community where all the usual Polish customs took place. One of the buildings was used as a church and priests would celebrate the religious festivals with the people. Father M. Lewendowski later replaced Father Ernest Choweuiec, who celebrated his twentieth anniversary in the priesthood at Foxley. No weddings took place in the camp, as the church did not have a license. Apparently in 1948 the Polish community was shocked by a double tragedy when Staff Sergeant Bogden Dziopinski shot his wife, Czeslawa, and then killed himself, leaving their young son an orphan.

'Icicle Execution' at Camp Foxley (H. Pavlovich).

The living accommodation for the Poles was the barracks, which stood in rows on either side of the road that led up the valley from Mansel Lacy to Yazor. Some barracks were set-aside for unmarried people as dormitories; others were converted to family units. Henry Pavlovich, a young boy at the time, remembers that each barrack was divided into accommodation or non-accommodation blocks. There were at least 400 housing units housing over 1,200 people. Henry's block number was 398. He recalls:

Primary School teachers at Mansel Lacy School (H.Pavlovich).

"Each living unit comprised a kitchen and three other rooms plus a toilet. A stove in one room had a stovepipe exiting through the roof. There were no bathrooms and people used tin tubs. There was no hot water. The bricks were large hollow things about four inches thick and 12 inches by 8 inches face on. The barracks were very cold."

Henry recalls that although the facilities were very basic at the camp at Foxley the setting was idyllic.

"There was a stream running down the valley towards a water station down near Mansel Lacy. The camp was surrounded by woods, which were one big playground for the kids as long as we didn't go too far in, and a source of food for adults who knew a lot about mushrooms (which were always ignored by English people). Parts of the camp still had the ruins of the old army buildings such as the boiler house and laundry (where as kids we used to find army buttons in the rubble)."

The community at Foxley had all the amenities of a rural village. There was a butcher's shop, which sold Polish food and a grocery van and fish van would visit the camp each week. The Poles could use the Post Office at

Mansel Lacy. There was also a cinema where Polish films were shown. The building used as a cinema was unheated so films were usually shown in the summer. There was also a licensed club known as the Rovers Club and an entertainment hall where an Anglo-Polish band sometimes played. A school was established in one of the barracks blocks, which became known as the Porto San Giorgio/Foxley School. It was used on Saturdays when the children would learn about the Polish language and culture. The school was named after the Porto San Giorgio area of Italy where the children had previously been taught.

When the Polish children were old enough they would attend the small primary school in Mansel Lacy. Mrs. Nowasielski remembers that her oldest child cried when she was old enough to attend school. She didn't speak English and she was worried because she didn't know how to ask for the toilet.

Picture sent to Aniela Dziuba in Canada (G. Weber).

The adults at Foxley were offered training in different trades like cobbling and carpentry and Henry Pavlovich remembers that a number of Poles made themselves a pair of hand lasted shoes before finding themselves jobs elsewhere. Some found jobs in factories locally, others moved away from the area. A number went to Birmingham to work in the automotive industry. Henry's father, Zbigniew Pawlowicz retook his qualifications in medicine and qualified as a psychiatric nurse, finishing his career teaching in psychiatric nursing.

A number of the Poles at Foxley chose to emigrate to America and Canada. Ginny Weber, a Canadian of Polish extraction, recently found in her mother's possessions a photo of two men taken at Foxley with a message in Polish on the back saying:

"Na palmate (a memento) *Foxley, nr. Hereford, Anglia maj 1948r."*

Ginny's mother, Aniela Dziuba, had been working in Germany as forced labour from 1940 until the end of the war. When the war ended she was working in the British Zone of Germany and was given the chance to emigrate. From Germany it's possible she sailed to the U.K. to stay at Foxley while the paperwork etc. was sorted out. She arrived in Canada as a displaced person in the autumn of 1947 and eventually settled in Winnipeg, Manitoba. Other families moved back to Poland when the situation was more settled there. The Michalaks moved back to Warsaw in 1948.

*Left - Mansel Lacy Church showing graves
of Poles who died at Foxley (M.Collins).
Right - Plaque in graveyard at Mansel Lacy displaying names
of Poles who died at Foxley (J.Stansbie).*

139

Chapter 16
FOXLEY HOUSING ESTATE

Horace (known as Joe) Bradbury, the water engineer for the U.S. hospitals at Foxley, had the opportunity to move his family to Foxley in 1948. The family moved into 'Engineer House'. This consisted of a brick built, single storey building containing kitchen, living room, three bedrooms and bathroom with large workshop and two offices attached. The family used one of the nissen huts as a garage. Joe's daughter, Susan, was very pleased to be moving there. She recalls:

"It was our first home with a water supply, inside toilet and electricity. Where we lived before was right out in the country. We were used to oil lamps and we collected all our water from the well across the road."

The Bradburys were the only English people at Foxley at that time except for one English girl, Sheila Duczakowski (later known as Dewing), who had married a Pole. Joe's wife, Doris got on very well with Sheila and they kept in touch long after they had both moved away from Foxley.

Joe's twin daughters, Jennifer and Susan remember playing in the empty wards before they were converted to apartments. Susan also remembers the Manor House, which was derelict when they moved to Foxley in 1948. She recalls that the garden was completely overgrown. Joe Bradbury had a key to the house so he could check on the water pressure etc. The girls would sometimes accompany him, although they did not dare venture upstairs. Susan remembers the expensive flock wallpaper in the house. Shortly after this the house was demolished as it was deemed a 'dangerous structure'. The two Bradbury girls attended Mansel Lacy Junior School. After Junior School it was necessary to travel further afield to the local secondary schools which were Weobley Secondary School, Hereford High School and Lady Hawkins Grammar School in Kington.

In 1950 Hereford Council took over responsibility for the estate and proposed to turn many of the derelict huts into living accommodation for homeless English people. Joe became the foreman for the camp and reported

Left - Susan Bradbury outside the Bradbury's home (S. Williams).
Right - Joe Bradbury in Special Constable Uniform (S. Williams).

to Hereford Council any need for repair or maintenance on the site. The council was concerned that the wooden Canadian huts situated near the Manor House would constitute a fire risk. Joe Bradbury proposed burning the overgrown grass on the land next to the huts with the supervision of the Fire Service to minimise the risk. There was much correspondence between Joe Bradbury and the Council officers. Joe also became the Special Constable for the estate while Doris, became the relief post woman and started a newspaper business from home, delivering papers and magazines.

Hereford City Council converted each hospital ward into seven self-contained homes, there were between three and four hundred altogether. Once the buildings were habitable the Poles moved into them and were joined by nearly 400 British homeless families who were glad to have a roof over their heads in the housing shortage immediately after the war. Most of these families were awaiting rehousing and chose to live at Foxley rather than share a home with in-laws or other family members.

The homes cost only 13 shillings a week to rent but were very basic. The rent man spent a day at Foxley each week. He set up his office in one of the houses and the residents paid their money through the open living room window.

Susan Bradbury with Polish homes in background (S. Williams).

Each home had an entrance hall, kitchen, living room and two or three bedrooms. The buildings had electricity and running water but no bathrooms. The showers were in a separate building and were not at all popular. Mrs. Nowasielski remembers that residents preferred to heat water on the stove to fill up a tin bath rather than go to the shower block. It was very difficult to decorate the buildings to make them more home-like. Some families stuck newspaper over the internal breeze-blocks and then stuck wallpaper on the top.

In 1952 two of the huts were converted into seven lock-up shops, a bus shelter and a public lavatory. In the same year the council planned to sell off some of the buildings not needed on the estate and also many of the fittings originally used by the Americans. Most of the Canadian huts were sold off at this point.

One of the ward buildings was bought and moved to Edwin Ralph, near Bromyard to serve as a village hall. On 6 October 1988 Dr. Tom Glennon visited the village and presented a plaque worded as follows:

"THIS BUILDING WAS
ORIGINALLY A HOSPITAL WARD
OF THE 123RD GEN. HOSP. U.S.A.
1944-1945
FOXLEY-MANSEL LACY."

Tom Glennon and Pamela Lee (V.Haines).

While visiting the area Dr. Glennon took the opportunity to visit his former hostess's daughter, Pamela Lee (nee Whiting).

Another hut from Foxley was bought and transported to Newent in Gloucestershire, about 25 k.m. southeast of Foxley. It was rebuilt and opened as Newent's Memorial Hall on April 4 1954 and is still there serving the same purpose today. In April 2004 the building celebrated its fiftieth anniversary with a gathering and rededication ceremony.

All who lived at Foxley after the war mention its strong sense of community. Henry Pavlovich remembers that people of other nationalities like Greeks and Italians also made their home at Foxley for a time. There was a tenants association with an English chairman, Polish secretary and a committee of six Poles and six Britons. In 1953 plans to celebrate Coronation Day at Foxley were prepared by Foxley Coronation Committee. It was necessary to request the Council to remove the stump and roots of a felled tree and the supports of the American flagstaff, which were sunk in concrete in the centre of a grassy expanse where the committee planned to hold a children's party.

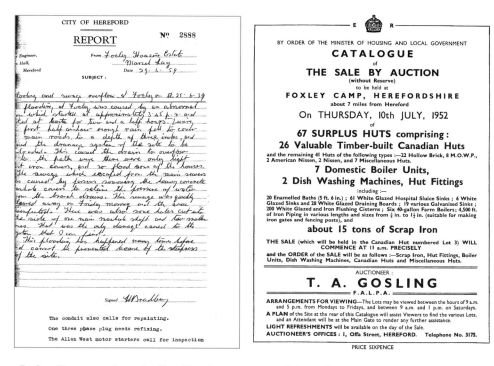

Left - Report written by Joe Bradbury on condition of sewers (Hereford Council).
Right - Sale catalogue cover for auction of 1952.

There was some petty thieving on the estate, perhaps the result of wartime shortages and probably not carried out by residents of Foxley. In March 1952 it was necessary for Joe Bradbury to report the robbery of an electric motor from the boiler house. After the police had inspected the scene of crime they requested Joe to nail up the entrance door. This he did, but the next morning he found that a second motor had been stolen.

A less serious incident was reported in April 1957 when one of the youngsters, Arthur Lyneham, got hurt on the barbed wire that prevented the residents from the housing estate, trespassing on the Davenport Estate. The Education Authority wrote to Major Davenport to complain that the barbed wire was dangerous and plain wire should be substituted but Major Davenport thought that the barbed wire should remain as it gave a clear message to 'keep out'. He obviously had very little sympathy for Arthur's plight as apparently Arthur had been picking daffodils on his land. Susan Williams (nee Bradbury), who went to school with Arthur, remembers that the woods were full of daffodils. She recalls:

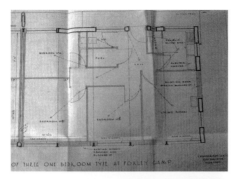
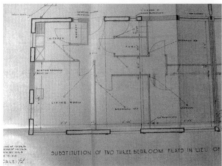

Left - Plans of 3 bedroomed flats 1951 (Hereford Council).
Right - Foxley Hall (H.Pavlovich).

"We were lucky, as dad had access to the private woods owned by Major Davenport as he had to 'walk the water pipes' to check for leaks etc. Our family was allowed unlimited access, although Major L avenport's sons did sometimes challenge us."

Around 1958 a number of Foxley families moved into Hereford as housing became available. Those remaining at Foxley were finding that the camp was beginning to disintegrate. The buildings were beginning to crumble and there were problems with overflowing sewers due to the steepness of the site and the temporary nature of the sewage facilities. As during the war, there were problems with rats. Eventually the rats outnumbered the residents and it was necessary for Hereford City Council's housing chairman, Sam Beaumont to make arrangements for the remainder of the residents to be re-housed in Hereford. The Bradburys were the last family to leave and in 1963 the site was demolished.

Epilogue
GONE, BUT NOT FORGOTTEN

The visitor to Foxley today would see few traces of the time when it was home to the peoples of a number of nations: Canada, America, France, Germany and Poland, not to mention its English residents.

In the woods the road still runs through the camp, linking the hut bases, which are all that are left of the wards and barracks. A stone stands adjacent to the road with a memorial to the personnel of the 123rd General Hospital who served there. Not far from the road several trees bear the names of Americans who were at the camp like 'Stubby' from Chicago.

Names of G.Is cut into trees at Foxley (M. Collins).

Names of G.Is cut into trees at Foxley (M. Collins).

Main Gate leading into Foxley Camp 2003 (M. Collins).

Roadway leading through Camp 2003 (M.Collins).

Hut bases clearly seen amongst trees 2003 (M. Collins).

Tom Glennon sums up what many who had lived there would wish for Foxley:

"Before the hospitals were built the site was just the park, green grass and trees, and in the spring, daffodils and primroses and cowslips were in abundance. Now, alas, huts have been built on the greensward and many cement walks have been cut through the place.

The necessities of war have crowded out the quiet and the beautiful. Perhaps when the last activities of World War Two have been completed, the area will again take its place as the broad park and quiet green of the old days. And only the memory of the thousands who have come and gone will linger in its sheltered acres. May we see it some day in all its recovered beauty and glory." The Officers Club - Thomas Glennon.

Memorial to the 123rd General Hospital (R. Michtom).

ABBREVIATIONS AND TERMS

ABBREVIATIONS

A.A. - Anti Aircraft

A.R.C. - American Red Cross

A.T.S. - Auxiliary Territorial Service

C.O. - Commanding Officer

C.47 - Dakota - 2 engined transport plane.

D.S.C. - Distinguished Service Cross - Award for valour/extraordinary heroism in military operations against an armed enemy.

E.E.N.T. - Ear, Eye, Nose and Throat

E.T.O. - European Theatre of Operations

M.T.O. - Mediterranean theatre of Operations.

P.T.O. - Pacific Theatre of Operations.

F.A. - Field Artillery

H.Q. - Headquarters.

I. and E. - Instruction and Education - towards the end of the war several schools were set up to help to educate G.Is to help them to gain qualifications before returning to the U.S.

L.C.V.P. - Landing Craft - Vehicle and Personnel

L.S.T. - Landing ship Tank

M.P. - Military Police

Naafi - Navy, Army, Air Force Institute. Main purpose to sell personal items to military personnel.

P.X. - Post Exchange - U.S. equivalent of Naafi.

N.C.O. - Non-commissioned Officer

O.D. - Olive Drab - usually referring to off duty uniform.

Pfc. - Private First Class

P.O.W. - Prisoner of War

R.A.F. - Royal Air force

R.C.A.F. - Royal Canadian Air Force.

W.A.A.F. - Women's Auxiliary Air Force.

W.V.S. - Women's Voluntary Service - British civilian organisation

U.S.O. - United Services Organisation - entertained G.Is during World War 2.

TERMS

Ambulatory - walking wounded.

Assigned - having Permanent duties at a base.

Limited Assignment - having temporary duties at a base.

Detached - detailed for Special Service.

Autoclave - closed vessel that allows the application of pressure and heat - used for sterilising surgical instruments.

Half and Half - half a pint of mild mixed with half a pint of bitter - a popular drink with the G.Is during World War II.

Long Toms - 155mm Howitzers

Mess hall - dining room

Operation Bolero - codename for movement of American troops to U.K. as a staging post for the Allied invasion of Europe.

Operation Overlord - Codename for Allied invasion of France.

Operation Torch - Codename for Allied invasion of North Africa.

Station Hospitals (S.H) - Hospitals with 834 beds serving the needs of troops in training.

General Hospitals (G.H.) - Hospitals with 1082 beds although at times it was necessary to fit in more patients. Intended for soldiers wounded during combat.

Convalescent Hospitals (C.H.) - treated convalescing troops sent from Station or General Hospitals.

Special Service - education and entertainment section responsible for morale of troops on a base.

Shooting Craps - dice game involving betting

Communication Zone - Area behind the combat zone- i.e. U.K.

Zone of the Interior - U.S.A.

APPENDIX 1

UNITS KNOWN TO HAVE BEEN AT FOXLEY

1940
2nd Canadian Pioneer Battalion

March 1944
22nd A.A. Artillery Group
203rd A.A. Artillery Battery A.W. Battalion
204th A.A. Artillery Battery A.W. Battalion
414th A.A. Artillery Gun Battalion
445th A.A. Artillery A.W.
519th A.A. Artillery Gun
553 Engineer Heavy Pontoon Battalion
602 Engineer Camouflage Battalion
749th Tank Battalion
1310th Engineer General Service Regiment.

June 1944
99th General Hospital
156th General Hospital

August 1944
123rd General Hospital

December 1944
408th F.A. Battalion
16th Tank Destroyer
292nd Field Artillery Observation Battalion
473rd Collection Company
548th F.A. Battalion
656th Tank Destroyer Battalion
768th Field Artillery Battalion

May 1945
377th M.P. Patrol Detachment
379th M.P. Patrol Detachment
380th M.P. Patrol Detachment

APPENDIX 2A

ARMY HOSPITAL CENTERS

Hospital Center	Hospital Group	Place	Date of Activation
12	5	Malvern	April 1944
15	4	Cirencester	April 1944
801	1	Taunton	Feb. 1945
802	2	Blandford	Feb. 1945
803	3	Devizes	Feb. 1945
804*	6	Whitchurch	Feb. 1945
805	7	Newmarket	Feb. 1945

N.B. Hospital Groups designated October 1944
Originally 6801 provisional-activated June 1944.

APPENDIX 2B

U.S. ARMY HOSPITALS IN U.K. AUGUST 1944

Plant No.	Site	Hospital Unit
4100	Truro	314SH
4101	Tavistock	115SH
4102	Moretonhampstead ?	
4103	Newton Abbot	124GH
4104	Exeter	36SH
4105	Barnstaple	313SH
4106	Bishops Lydeard	185GH
4107	Norton Manor	101GH
4108	Taunton	67GH
4109	Axminster	315SH
4110	Yeovil, Houndstone	169GH
4111	Yeovil, Lutton	121GH
4112	Sherborne	228SH
4113	Frome St Quintin	305SH
4114	Blandford	22GH
4115	Blandford	119GH
4116	Blandford	125GH
4117	Blandford	131 GH
4118	Blandford	140GH
4119	Wimborne	106GH
4120	Ringwood	104GH
4121	Netley	110SH
4122	Winchester	38SH
4123	Stockbridge	34GH
4124	Odstock	158GH
4125	Grimsdith	250SH
4126	Waronnster	216GH
4127	Tidworth	3SH
4128	Perharn Downs	103GH
4129	Everleigh	187GH
4130	Devizes	141GH
4131	Devizes	128GH

4132	Erlestoke Park	102GH
4133	Bath	160SH
4134	Falfield	94GH
4135	Malmesbury	120SH
4136	Lydiard Park	302SH
4137	Swindon	154GH
4138	Chiseldon	130SH
4139	Marlborough	347SH
4140	Hermitage	98GH
4141	Checkendon	306GH
4142	Kingwood	304GH
4143	Wheatley	97GH
4144	Headington	91GH
4145	Middleton Stoney	318SH
4146	Ramsden	317SH
4147	Burford	61GH
4148	Fairford	186GH
4149	Cirencester	188GH
4150	Cirencester	192GH
4151	Daglinworth	1 1lGH
4152	Stowell Park	160GH
4153	Ullenwood	110GH
4154	Blockley	327SH
4155	Moreton	
4156	Fairford	
4157	Salisbury	152SH
4165	Tyntesfield	74GH
4166	Bristol	117GH
4167	Stoneleigh	307SH
4168	Bromsgrove	123SH
4169	Wolverley	52GH
4170	Bewdley	297GH
4171	Bewdley	114GH
4172	Blackmore Park	93GH
4173	Blackmore Park	155GH
4174	MalvernWells	96GH
4175	Malvern Wells	53GH
4176	Malvern Wells	55GH
4177	Leominster	135GH

4178	Foxley	123GH
4179	Foxley	156GH
4180	Kington	122GH
4181	Kington	107GH
4182	Abergavenny	279SH
4183	Rhyd Lafar	81GH
4184	Carmarthen	232SH
4185	Lichfield	33SH
4186	Shugborough	312SH
4187	Sudbury Derby	182GH
4188	Whittington	68GH
4189	Oteley Deer Park	137GH
4190	Overton	83GH
4191	Penley	129GH
4192	Iscoyd Park	82GH
4193	Saighton	109GH
4194	Clatterbridge	157GH
4195	Stockton Heath	168SH
4196	Davey Hulme	10SH
4197	Glasgow	316SH
4198	Harrogate	115GH
4199	Harrogate	116GH
4200	Mansfield	184GH
4201	Nocton Hall	7GH
4202	Allington	348SH
4203	Thorpe North	303SH
4204	Diddington	49SH
4205	Cambridge	163GH
4206	Newport	280SH
4207	Braintree	121SH
4208	Acton, Suffolk	136SH
4209	Redgrave Park	65GH
4210	Wymondham	231SH
4211	North Minuns	IGH
4212		
4213	Packington	77SH
4261	London	16SH

APPENDIX 3

TRAINS ARRIVING AT MOORHAMPTON STATION
WITH PATIENTS FOR FOXLEY

Date	Type of Train	Departed from
28/09/1944	OAT 14	Chiseldon
23/10/1944	OAT 14	Netley
3/11/1944	OAT 14	Chiseldon
26/11/1944	HAT 1	Newbury Racecourse
7/12/1944	HAT 65	Southampton
18/02/1945	HAT 72	Southampton
20/02/1945	HAT 72	Southampton
5/03/1945	HAT 72	Chiseldon

HAT - Home Ambulance Train

OAT - Overseas Ambulance Train

11th March 1944 - 2 trains arrived at Moorhampton from Glasgow -
  possibly bringing personnel from one of the artillery units.

28th July 1944 - 99 G.H. departed by train from Moorhampton
  to Llandudno.

29th July 1944 - 2 trains arrived at Moorhampton from Glasgow bringing
  the 123rd G.H.

ACKNOWLEDGEMENTS

In grateful acknowledgement of the following people and sources:

G.B.
M. Atkin, Thelma Beresford, Betty Children, Major David Davenport, Charles Evans, Linda Goodwin, Vivienne Haines, Phil and Hazel Highley, Marian Maczka, Mrs. Nowasielski Marjorie Kent Phillips, Mark Simmons, Doreen Skinner, William H. Smith, John Stansbie, Adrian and Neil Turley, Eileen Walters, Mike Webster, Susan Williams.

U.S./Canada
George Baker, Carl McDaniel, Edna Jo Fecht, Robert Kauffman, Robert Masters, Robert J. Michtom, Gordon Mize, Ray Olsen, Lilian Ostrand, Richard O. Penick, Charles and Richard Rzeszutko, Dave Stofer, Walt Venema, Ginny Weber, Beverley J. Wilbert, Leo Wisniewski, Mary Zeller.

Other Publications and Institutions
Hereford Times
Robin Hill and Hereford Library
SMR Herefordshire County Council
The American Legion Magazine
The V.F.W. Magazine
Shaef Communique
Bulge Bugle
749er
Webpage: 749th Tank Battalion Training in Texas and England
  - David Heathcott
Readers Digest
548th F.A. Battalion From Activation to Victory in Europe
National Archives and Records Administration:
  History of 12th Hospital Center
  History of 99th General Hospital
  History of 123rd General Hospital
  History of 156th General Hospital
  History of A.R.C. at 123rd General Hospital
  History of A.R.C. at 156th General Hospital